I0221770

A First-Time Founder's Guide to Hiring Exceptional People

RECRUIT THE REMARKABLE

J. Patrick Gorman

ISBN 979-8-9900320-0-2

*To my parents, who taught me to stay humble,
think global, and act with integrity.*

*To my son, who allows me to enjoy the wonder
of childhood all over again.*

To NYC and its unbeatable energy.

To Brazil and its unforgettable soul.

CONTENTS

PROLOGUE

Personality drives leadership, leadership drives
organizational performance, and who is in charge
matters greatly for the fate of organizations and
the people in them.
—Dr. Robert Hogan

Leadership is not about attributes, it's about behavior.
—John Kotter

Congratulations, Founder. You had the courage to start your
own business. This act alone is remarkable. You are embark-
ing on a path of leadership that many people talk about but
seldom ever take the first step.

As a newbie, everyone from grandmas to gurus are going to
share their opinions on how to make your vision real.

Here's mine: The most important skill you can master is
safeguarding the consistency of your company's culture.

Culture is the collective behavior of you and your team.
Consistent, quality behavior is practiced by those professionals
who are self-aware, self-motivated, and committed to excellence. Typically, this type of professional is referred to as a

"game-changer" or a "rock star".

This book is going to teach you how to recruit the best of the best.

If it were easy to get these stars "on the bus" during the initial stages of your startup, everybody would do it. No one would need my services, and certainly no one would need this book.

I know it is a *struggle*.

Most founders learn how to recruit through trial and error. They spend months and months navigating the endless maze of LinkedIn. For weeks (and weeks) they suffer through unnecessary coffee chats and the cruelty of counteroffers until they earn their stripes and figure out how to recruit effectively.

The better way is to value your time over money.

We pay for every lesson with either time or money.
And we use the currency we value least.
—Alex Hormozi

I wrote *Recruit the Remarkable* for those founders who value time more than money. Put in the time now, absorb the lessons in this book, and then enjoy the rewards of hiring better and faster.

Revisit this book's lessons as needed, so that the methods I teach you become instinctive: your routine, your standard, your culture. In the end, learning how to hire well makes all the difference in creating a company culture that consistently delights your customers, builds trust with your partners, and cements your brand's legacy.

We'll begin with broad lessons on mindset and then shift to specific hiring tactics you can implement at your startup.

It is my sincere hope that the twenty-plus years of lessons I have learned from recruiting for Silicon Valley–backed companies,

Wall Street legends, and unicorn tech founders will inspire you to reframe the struggle of recruiting into a valuable opportunity to grow. Grow in a way that will help you identify, engage, and successfully hire the very best team for your startup company.

INTRODUCTION

8:03 a.m.
Monday, February 5, 2007
New York, NY

My business partner, Jodi, and I sat anxiously in our shared office space high above Fifth Avenue.

The two of us had just left a large, well-known head-hunting agency to start our own recruitment firm. Our nervous energy could have powered half of Manhattan's homes that day.

Suddenly, Jodi's cellphone rang. She picked up and pitched; we listened and waited.

Hanging up the phone, her smile grew wide. "We have our first client."

"Who?" I asked.

"Goldman Sachs."

Talk about pressure.

It was an exhilarating start for us. We had just signed the world's preeminent investment bank as our first client. Kudos to my partner for a job well done. We were off to the races.

You can only imagine the standards that Goldman had, especially when agreeing to pay our fees to help them attract talent to their world headquarters. Couple that with the anxiety we felt as first-time founders. It was stressful to say the least.

From this fortunate start, we began to apply the lessons of recruiting we had learned from our previous employer, as well as our own personal experiences, to complete the bank's mandates. Shortly thereafter, more clients came calling, including founders of hedge funds, KKR, Morgan Stanley, 3G, Blackstone, and other luminaries of Wall Street.

The next five years were a wild and invaluable experience with the financial titans of New York. But then it was time for the next chapter in my life. I sold my equity stake to my partner and made a personal decision to move my family to Brazil. There, I set up shop in São Paulo—the 12-million-person epicenter for technology companies in Latin America. In Brazil, I shifted my focus from founders of investment partnerships to founders of tech startups. Many of the tech clients I helped in their early startup days are now unicorns ($1 billion+ USD valuation). Observing firsthand how those tech founders hired, scaled, and behaved was an invaluable learning experience.

And now I get to share those same lessons with you.

But so what? There are all kinds of books out there related to hiring talent. Why would my story matter to you?

Because I, too, have been a first-time founder.

Because I've had to find product-market fit.

Because I've had to hire a team to attend to extraordinarily selective clients.

Because I've signed a ten-year lease guaranteed by my personal assets in case I couldn't pay the monthly rent for high-end Midtown Manhattan office space.

Because I've felt the highest of highs with big placements and fees in 2007 as well as the acute stress and anxiety when revenue fell off a cliff during the Great Recession of 2008–2009.

Because I became a first-time dad in the middle of that same financial crisis.

I share this background so you'll know the content here is not only from a fellow founder but has been stress-tested—professionally and personally.

Just in case you're not convinced, shortly after starting my second headhunting company in Brazil I got divorced.

Ever been a single dad in a non-English-speaking country running a business helping Silicon Valley–backed startups hire their founding teams?

I'm not an amateur. I have been there. I know crazy.

In simple, straightforward terms, let's master the core principles and processes to ensure *you* recruit at your best to attract the best.

Remember, great founders are great recruiters.

Here's how they do it.

PART ONE

THE FOUR CORE FACTORS

Chapter 1
UNTOUCHABLE

Everything else can be taken from you, but this power to choose what you think, what you remember, and what you believe about yourself is untouchable.
—Dr. Nate Zinsser

To the outside world, you are confident and bold, a risk-taker. As a founder, you must be all those things.

But on the inside, how do you feel?

To be a magnet for elite talent, you must start by examining the roots of your self-belief. Ask yourself, *What does my self-talk sound like?*

Is it consistently reminding you that you can achieve anything you set your mind to (e.g. convince Naval Ravikant to join your startup)? Or is it working against you as your own harshest critic (*She runs a division of Airbnb and went to Stanford; she won't be interested in joining us*)?

You won't be able to recruit the best if you succumb to self-sabotage. To change course and realign, let me describe what self-confidence looks like.

First, self-confidence is posture.

Posture is more than just the proverbial "stand up straight." It is *voice tone*—an awareness of your voice as an instrument. When you speak to me, do I feel your self-confidence?

It is that burning truth behind *your gaze*. When you look at me, will I believe in your company's vision? When you look in the mirror, is it there?

It is in *human touch*, felt from how you shake hands to how you embrace a team member after a huge win or a devastating loss.

Second, self-confidence is a pledge to the preciousness of time.

Confident founders say "no" quickly and easily. Saying "yes" is a show of true commitment; it means they're "all in." And forget about "maybes." Great founders won't entertain the potential waste of a "maybe."

Maybes never are.
—Anne McCaffrey, *Dragonsong*

To recruit at your best, your "yes" is a commitment, a bond. Your "yes" does not skip that coffee, miss that call, or delay that interview. Your "yes" is indistractable.

Lastly, self-confidence is kind, not nice.

The best founders are not "nice guys and gals." They are never concerned about fitting in with the cool crowd. They are purpose-driven and lead with positive intent. They make tough calls and don't apologize for it. More importantly, they don't ruminate over a decision after making it.

They possess posture.

Yes, I am back to that word "posture." When you commit and embody posture, attracting star executives becomes easier since your essence mirrors theirs. Like them, you were never ordinary either.

In short, "posture" is your vibe.

When you bring that juice, that oxygen, to how you move, speak, and interact with a game-changing executive, recruiting them to your startup becomes effortless.

"Effortless? Give me a break, Patrick. I am not here to read another woo-woo, self-help book about 'faking it before making it.' Tell me how to recruit already!"

I get it. Maybe you are rolling your eyes reading my counsel to feed your mind (and heart) a steady diet of self-belief to recruit at your best.

Go ahead, skip this step.

Do it your way.

I dare you.

Bypassing the "work" to become self-assured is a gamble. Sure, you may get lucky and recruit a rock-star CFO here or an elite CTO there, but the truth is you won't be able to do it consistently.

As a founder, I recognize you feel alive when someone tells you that you cannot do something. It energizes you to do things your way and prove them wrong. It is in your DNA to go against the grain.

But in this case, I want you to resist that urge. Don't skip this step. You can still choose to ignore my advice, but like gambling, eventually the house of bad hires will win.

Remember: In practice, like attracts like.

As you know like attracts like, if you want
better people in your life, you must work on
being a better person yourself.
—Leon Brown

All I am asking you to do is copy how star talents already act. They habitually work on their mindset so that their indefatigable self-belief becomes self-evident.

You will get there too. Once you do, it will be easy to attract a culture of people who stand out from the pack, continuously and consistently. Why? Because you are just like them. Like attracts like.

Now wouldn't that be a nice problem to have?

The winning formula starts with confidence then moves to honing competence.[1]

Competence comes through practicing the tactics I'll detail later in this book. For now, know that I can only mold you into an elite recruiter when you commit to self-belief.

KEY TAKEAWAY

The right mindset is felt by others through:
1. Practicing the trifecta of self-belief: body language, voice tone, and eye contact.
2. Mastering this trifecta so that each interaction with star executives feels unforgettable.
3. Being unforgettable wins their hearts and sets the stage for your deliberate, well-executed recruitment process to bring them onboard.
4. The order of "confidence then competence" is an unbeatable combination to recruit the best.

---

1 Credit to Dr. Nate Zinsser for this confident + competent model.

Chapter 2
LISTEN TO LEARN

A well-known entrepreneur introduced me to a senior leader at one of Silicon Valley's most famous venture capital funds. On the call, this executive shared with me his best advice for startup founders: become a great storyteller. Learning how to captivate the listener is what he saw as the highest priority skill for founders to develop.

For most of us, that counsel makes a lot of sense. But for founders who want to master recruiting elite talent, it's the wrong message.

Here's the right one.

Look, storytelling matters. How you pitch to incubators like Y-Combinator, or your first group of Silicon Valley venture capitalists or Wall Street investors, etc. I get it—it matters.

However, to recruit at your best, what matters *more* is understanding who is sitting across from you.

What story do *they* want to tell? And, more importantly, are you actively listening for it?

Let's have a tangible example to best illustrate my point. Imagine you are a first-time founder who has experienced fantastic growth. Product is being shipped out and customer checks are coming in. Demands on your time are at an all-time high. On a Sunday morning looking over last month's results you realize you are *spent*. Sundays cannot be absorbed by organizing the books, records, taxes, and monthly budget. You need to hire; you need help.

It is time to recruit your first CFO.

Yes, your startup has an attractive story, but how you tell it depends on what matters to the CFO candidates who will soon be sitting across from you. To understand what matters to them, design questions that unearth their values and motives. Here are some examples to get you started:

- What piqued your interest in meeting with me today?
- When did you realize you were unique in finance?
- Which professor will you never forget? Which one would you like to forget?
- Which professional mentor do you return to time and time again when you need sound advice?
- What would your high school friends tell me you will be doing at fifty? Are you on that path?
- If not, how did you veer off course?

The conversation sounds almost like a first date. And in a way, it is. To build your leadership team you are looking for a "marriage" where you share similar values.

You cannot understand one's values if you don't engage in active listening. Active listening is when you focus on understanding the incredible story they want to tell you about themselves.

What do they value, what motivates them, and what do they want?

In summary, you are asking them to tell you who they are

and where they want to go to feel fulfilled in their life story.

"Great Patrick, I will listen really hard, but what is your point? I don't have time to listen to why they love the color green."

My point is simple: it is *their* story that matters, *not yours*.

No other founder is going to ask questions to understand the fabric of this CFO's life, except you.

Instead, most founders will continue to be average at recruiting because they will single-mindedly focus on what their company needs first rather than understanding the motives and values of the star executive sitting in front of them.

Most founders will get stuck in matching the technical skills of the candidate to the job description rather than knowing whether there is a cultural fit through deep listening to the candidate's life story.

Don't get me wrong, the technical nature of an interview is important. Making sure the executive will fit the job description is essential.

However, when recruiting the Michael Jordan of finance, you have to start with creating an environment that will allow him to open up about what he thinks is truly important. The "thing" that moves him is rarely a line on the balance sheet. More likely it is his adopted cat, his annual ski trip with his mates, or the reason he prefers the color green. (Isn't money green?)

To be the best listener, you have to genuinely show interest in that cat, that ski trip, that color.

Most founders won't care about the cat. I get it, but if you wanted to be just another founder you would not be reading this book.

Moving on.

Let's expand on a critical skill: being an exceptional listener.

How to Be an Exceptional Listener

To get the most out of interviews, internalize the following tactics:

1. **Be a blank slate.** Don't assume you know what the executive is going to say.
2. **Listen without thinking about what you want to say next.** Focus on who this person is and not on what can they do for you now.
3. **Moderate pace.** No one has all day. However, allow the conversation to flow along the path the star executive is creating. You may be surprised by what you learn (good and bad).
4. **Don't correct small details that don't really matter.** If he says that your favorite sports team's jersey color is green and it is blue, let it go. Maybe the star executive is color blind.
5. **Practice the improv comedy method.** When the star candidate ends a sentence and it's your turn to talk, repeat the last thing they said to you. By echoing their words, they will feel heard.

Employ these five techniques to understand nuance and grasp what truly matters to the star executive sitting in front of you. Remember, other founders won't listen like this. They won't pick up the subtle details that really matter.

By doing this, you will set yourself apart.

And once you know what matters to the executive, it is easy to decide if your company, the role, and its mission are a match.

If it is a good fit, offer specific examples of how your company's culture, team, and roles align with this star executive's life plans.

Tell them your story their way to hire the best.

Chapter 3
UNAPOLOGETIC

"Fake it until you make it" doesn't work.

This is not auditioning for a play. This is not a Hollywood movie. You are building a real company and affecting real people's lives.

How you act affects everything.

Recently, I was introduced to a first-time founder. She wanted my help to build her leadership team. Calling my network, I discovered she did not have a good reputation for people management.

At first, I was excited to work with her because of her first-class background and star-studded investor list. Also, I believe in giving everyone the benefit of the doubt, especially since I made many mistakes myself as a first-time founder. (I still make mistakes!)

Even though my source warned me about this founder's lack of management skills, I set up the meeting with her to listen to her side of the story as well as share the feedback I received about her substandard reputation for people management.

When I shared the feedback, her response told me everything I needed to know. Instead of giving me examples of staff people who would defend her people skills, management ability, and conscientious leadership, she told me that her investors had done their due diligence on her and that they invested.

Her point of view was that these big-time investors did their research on her, and they were comfortable she could manage the business well.

This response confirmed my fears. It signaled the wrong mindset for managing others.

Investors may say that they care about a leader's people skills but oftentimes what they *really* care about is the financial return made for their limited partners (i.e., investors).

How many venture capitalists backed controversial founders (e.g., FTX, Theranos, WeWork, etc.) because the focus was (and many times continues to be) on making money?

There is nothing wrong with making money, but great founders don't fake it. They embrace that being a founder requires a genuine people commitment. Their care for their team's well-being *as well as* their investors' interests is sincere.

This mentality carries over to recruiting. Recruiting is best performed by those founders who are committed to giving to others. It is a relationship they enter to give—which, when done well, ends up *bringing* immeasurable and unforgettable experiences to the founder.

Bringing us back to the founder I met with, what I wanted to see were examples where her staff was defending her leadership style and vouching for her reputation. Instead, I got the commercial vibe of "my investors know everything about me, and they invested in me. That's what matters most."

"What are you really trying to say here, especially as it relates to me recruiting the best talent for my startup? Cut to the chase, please!"

It is easy to attract top talent when you have star investors and a great product. But if you don't learn how to genuinely lead with both skill *and* benevolence, it will be very difficult to retain this talent and, subsequently, recruit their valuable network of first and second connections.

In the end, I trust that this founder will eventually learn to be a better listener. If she does not commit to this path, then she should step out of her CEO role and promote another person dedicated to its demands. If she stays in her role, and does not adapt, she will lose good people, and odds are the company won't survive.

In summary, save yourself from recruiting heartache and retention problems by becoming sincerely interested in your people first. Don't fake it. Prioritize your people and watch the returns from your ***leadership*** behavior come rolling in.

KEY TAKEAWAY

Be curious about others. It shows your human touch.

Your human touch will be felt not only in your recruiting process but also by your incumbent team. Creating this environment, this culture where you *actually* put people first will inspire your team to recruit at their best.

Remember, everyone wants to work with people they admire, and everyone respects the person, the team, and the culture that is *unapologetically real.*

It is walking the talk.

It is genuine. It is rare.

When your actions speak louder than words you cannot help but attract the best.

Chapter 4
THE HERE AND NOW

7:17 a.m.
THE LOCAL CAFÉ

FOUNDER 1
How's work?

FOUNDER 2
Tough. We have to hire better, but our product is finally gaining traction. One of my investors just introduced me to Sheila, and I am jazzed. She's a Harvard MBA, former McKinsey manager, and now in her second year at Amazon. I'm meeting her here tomorrow and have a feeling she is going to be the best hire ever. Our mutual friend is a Venture Capitalist and he introduced us. What a background she has and, for sure, she will know other people we can hire to take us to unicorn status faster than we could have imagined.

FOUNDER 1
(privately resentful he *is not meeting Sheila)*
Good for you, man. If she is not a fit, let me meet her. Maybe we have a role for her on my team. It's so hard to meet people

like her and equally hard to recruit them. I would love to meet her too.

FOUNDER 2
(privately skeptical that Founder 1 will recruit Sheila from him now or in the future)
Sounds good. Changing gears, when is the next kitesurfing retreat with our VC?

This type of founder chat is happening right now all over the world. It is the proverbial "war for talent" that first-time founders feel when they don't embrace the lessons within this book.

The fact is that there are plenty of top MBAs with a background in consulting and experience with big companies like Amazon. Plenty.

The issue is that most of these "big company" managers are not right for the phase in which your company is in now.

Learn to resist the glamour of Harvard, McKinsey, and Amazon. I understand the allure. Their brand marketing is sexy. Yet, not everyone who attends these fine institutions has the right DNA for your startup. In other words, not everyone at McKinsey is "smart" for what your startup needs *now*.

Returning to the café chat scenario, neither of these founders has even met Sheila in person. She may only be taking the meeting with Founder 2 because she feels bad saying no to a coffee chat initiated by their VC friend in common.

Now let's say Sheila really wants to work at a startup and is willing to leave her big company and big brand name background to do so. But just because she wants to doesn't mean she has the profile to be successful in a company that does not have the budgets, the processes, nor the defined structures of McKinsey and Amazon.

Sheila may say she wants to join a startup, but what is her financial situation? Does she have a mortgage to pay, need specific healthcare benefits, or support an elderly parent and so prioritizes a good salary and regular working hours? Does she have $100K in MBA debt that Amazon is paying for? If she leaves for your startup, will it now become your liability?

As for her enticing contacts, are all her friends in the same boat? You assume she will introduce you to her high-quality, smart friends. But maybe all of them are risk-averse and destined to fail in your rough and tumble, Wild West startup environment that is going from 0 to 1.[2]

"Okay, Patrick, I get it. Just because someone has an incredible academic background and top professional employment names on their CV does not mean they are going to thrive at my 0 to 1 startup. Tell me something I don't already know."

I hear you. I just want to make sure you focus on their personality and skill set and not be overly impressed by their imposing, brand-name CV.

Let's move on to my second point.

Establish your recruiting focus based on what your business needs now.

When I talk about "what the business needs now," I am referring to the next one to five months.

When starting out and trying to establish product market fit, onboard multiple paying customers, and scale to provide stellar service, you need to look to hire for the qualities of agility, resourcefulness, and doing more with less.

---

2 The phrase "going from 0 to 1" was made famous by Peter Thiel, cofounder of PayPal. It means to build something from nothing to something.

The classic error startup founders make is to hire overqualified candidates who are mismatched for the early stage of their business's life cycle.

Don't be like everyone else. Keep reading. Get better.

Let's think through *why* hiring the overqualified executive usually does not work. Imagine the Amazon manager who has a hundred people under her command. She is used to a very specific structure and process, from how meetings are run to how performance is graded, as well as how hiring and firing work. Everything is in an outline, a structure for her to follow.

Don't believe me? Type "Jeff Bezos knows how to run a meeting" in Google Search and see how detailed the Amazon meeting process is.

Bezos built a system—a machine that works well because it follows a repeatable, defined process efficiently. Just follow the instructions and press play.

Most likely, your startup does not have such structure. You are still building the airplane mid-flight. As such, those executives who are used to flying according to an instruction manual are more often not a fit for the early stages of your startup. They are good at following rules, not making them up as they go along.

In summary, the lesson is to recruit for what your business needs now. Avoid the temptation to hire that star executive who has never scaled/operated in the frenetic environment your business currently finds itself in.

"Got it. Resist the glamour of CVs and the pull of those big company names. But how do I actually recruit for the *right* startup profile?"

I've got you covered. Let's get tactical.

Pre-Recruitment Brainstorming

The savvy startup founder asks two key questions before starting an interview process:

1. What problem does my business need resolved now?
2. What specific competence do I need now that once applied will crush this problem over the next few months?

Let's imagine that your challenge is your books and records. They are a mess, making it excruciatingly difficult to build reliable forecasts, budgets, and financial statements for outside investors. In this scenario, it is quite possible that your scrappy team has someone onboard who can quickly learn accounting and deliver a "good enough" budgeting process or financial model to show investors.

As such, the two pivotal questions above stimulate a savvy founder to reflect on and address (a) what the specific challenge actually is, and (b) if there is someone who can get the problem solved internally. Oftentimes, you won't need to hire outside help. Lean on your resourcefulness to see if you can delegate internally rather than hire externally.

In a scenario where no one on your team can deliver what your business needs now, then the answer is obvious: you need to start interviewing.

Before you start cranking out midnight LinkedIn messages to the Sheila Harvard MBA crowd, slow down and take five minutes to create a hiring plan. Here are two key components:

1. List the 2–3 specific skills needed to resolve the problem rapidly.

Remember, in the startup phase you need someone who can contribute immediately. Of course, there needs to be time for them to adapt, understand expectations, and jell with you and your team. However, that timeline needs to be short-term. Think in terms of weeks not months for evaluating any executive's skill set.

2. Do not fall into the trap of "this person will learn on the job."

Often this happens when interviewing top MBAs who have little, if any, startup experience. They will say all the right things in an interview about their desire to build something, feel part of a mission, build a legacy, take on the world, etc. But the fact remains: they are untested in the startup world. They also may be too soft to flourish in its ups and downs.

(Take it easy, top MBA from Bain. I am not saying that people like you cannot be great hires! I am simply making first-time founders aware of the risk in hiring you. Top consultants like you are overachievers, hard workers, and hyper-intelligent. But the fact is, many of you don't want to adapt to the realities of the "do more with less" startup. It is hard, unglamorous, and the odds are the company will fail and you will not make any money. Most people would not embark on such a risky career option especially when saddled with MBA school debt, a mortgage, and young kids at home. I get it and deeply respect those who stay in more traditional careers.)

"OK, it's clear. Focus on specific skills and don't assume they can learn on the job. But let's say we meet a top MBA and really think she has the specific skills to resolve our problem over the next 2–3 months and can hit the ground running on Day 1. Is there anything else? I don't want to make a hiring mistake."

Yes, follow the advice of legendary investor Martin Escobari: *Look for the person who has an extra oxygen tank.*

You want to look for grit, toughness, not giving up. That kind of resourceful problem-solver is easily identified in other tech startups but not so much within top consulting firms, Big Tech companies, or investment banks.

To find that "extra oxygen tank" person, focus your reference checks[3] on their ability to get results, problem solve, and show perseverance during *tough* projects. *Seek tangible examples from others* that this candidate has delivered work projects with the right attitude and fortitude for what your startup needs in the short term. The emphasis here is on asking others if this executive has that drive. You cannot rely on your impression when interviewing them face to face. Be as objective as possible and rely on the opinion of those who worked with him or her in the past.

Why?

Because interviewing is acting.

Brad Pitt CTO? Absolutely.

In person, I have no doubt Mr. Pitt could convince you he could run IT for your startup. Will Ferrell for Head of Sales and Morgan Freeman to replace you as CEO. All joking aside, unless you can get this person to work a trial period, rely on testing for that grit and resilience in the reference check to make better hiring decisions.

Simply put, the nature of a startup is uncertainty, adaptability, and velocity. Be accountable to this reality when evaluating talent. (Check out Ben Horowitz's book *The Hard Thing about Hard Things* as inspiration for this viewpoint.)

---

3 In future chapters I will detail how to conduct a proper reference check. For now, just remember two key points. Reference checks are more important than the interview. And never skip the step of performing a reference check, especially for your key leadership hires.

Characteristically, your best hires will have previously worked in the type of low-budget, high-volatility startup company that you founded.

They have seen this phase before and are going to know how to act, organize, experiment, and thrive under this kind of pressure.

Additionally, they have delivered on the specific short-term need that your business must resolve *now*.

Later, as your company grows both in revenue and head count, then consider adding those skilled Amazon, Microsoft, and Accenture managers who know how to lead efficient and effective teams at scale.

KEY TAKEAWAY

Big tech and big consulting managers know how to manage but rarely will they find seventeen ways to get out of jail without the keys.

Focus on hiring for what your early-stage business needs in the next few months, not in year 2 or 3. In many cases, you should hire those who have done a jailbreak before (figuratively speaking).

Keep in touch with "Sheila MBA." Recognize her talent but also know that she is probably not a good fit for now. Certainly, she is not someone you and your founder friends should be fighting over.

Of course, it's sexy to tell your investors and friends that your team is full of Harvard MBAs and Amazon folks. But no one will care about this if your company is not able to sell its product.

Not even your mom. Well, maybe your mom.

PART TWO

THE FIVE STEPS TO RECRUITING THE REMARKABLE

n the previous chapters we covered how important mindset, confidence, and posture are to becoming elite at recruitment.

We then chatted about how to become the best listener these star candidates have ever met and how doing so elevates your startup's interview experience to be remarkable. Nothing beats feeling listened to and understood.

Finally, we emphasized the importance of the here and now, assessing if the star executive can do what your startup needs in the short-term and resisting the seductive CV of that Ivy League MBA or BCG consultant who has never worked 0 to 1 before.

Now, we delve into the nuts and bolts.

For those of you who are the creative-type founder who drinks too much caffeine, you have been warned—we are going to talk here about process. Better refill that cup of joe and pay attention.

Process? Yes, process.

I expect most of you to want to glaze over this part of the book. Resist diverting yourself and power through these important procedural steps to recruit top talent.

As you'll find, it will be well worth your focus.

Chapter 5

BATTER UP
MAKING FIRST CONTACT

Management is doing things right;
leadership is doing the right things.
—Peter Drucker

How you initially contact a star candidate matters. When done well it sets the tone for an outstanding recruitment experience, ensuring star executives arrive and thrive on the job.

To be truly elite at recruiting, start with the right pitch.

Pitching to the Stars

All first-time founders can relate. Recruiting can be exhausting and frustrating. You invest so much of your time and effort to recruit that star CTO and, in the end, she turns down your offer.

Eventually, most founders learn how to recruit through trial and error. But what if there was a way to accelerate your learning and save time and effort?

There is.

It begins with how you stage that first contact with a star executive.

Stage? Yes, *stage*. I chose that word specifically.

You are not acting. What you will be doing is interacting. However, like an accomplished actor, I need you to prepare a pitch that requires focus, a lot of practice, and a dash of patience. Step into that aforementioned confident mindset.

You got this. You are this person. Own the feeling.

Next, avoid a common error. Don't present your pitch to star candidates in the same way you'd fundraise from VC investors.

Think about it. Is your current pitch to candidates identical to how you fundraise from investors? *If yes, you are doing it all wrong.*

Rarely will your pitch deck's data points be the reason a star executive comes on board. Do you really believe your CTO reminisces about joining your startup because she could not resist your unit economics? Or your first HR leader said yes as soon as he learned about your total addressable market stats (TAM)?

I am not saying that first-time founders shouldn't carefully craft how they pitch to investors. Rehearsing (and re-rehearsing) how to respond to investors' questions about product, go-to-market strategy, and growth projections is vitally important.

What I *am* saying is when recruiting star executives, take a different approach.

"OK, you want us to pitch candidates differently than investors, but how?"

Don't worry; I've got you covered.

7 Tips to Fast-Track Hiring the Best

Tip #1—Put Away Your Pitch Deck

Recruiting star executives isn't fundraising, it's matchmaking.

"What do you mean 'matchmaking'? I am not getting married here. I just need a strong CTO to help us grow."

Yeah, I hear you, but there are similarities. In recruiting, like marriage, you are asking another human being to embark with you on a journey that brings with it an emotional roller coaster. The big picture is wonderful, but it also includes a daily practice of commitment to scale something that can fail at least 50 percent of the time. Whether in love or at work, your potential partner must feel a connection to you *and* your cause.

Envision how Christopher Columbus recruited his first boat captain. There was a lot of pressure on him to get the right guy to captain that ship, literally. Queen Isabella of Spain was a pretty important investor. Just imagine her expectations of Columbus. Talk about pressure to get the right crew leader onboard!

Did Columbus sell prospects on how rich they would become? How famous they would be? How powerful they would be in the eyes of the Queen after completing the mission? Or did Columbus appeal to their sense of adventure with a journey over an unknown ocean to discover a new world?

We may never know how Columbus "closed the deal." Undoubtedly, he created *connection* with the boat captain candidate to receive his commitment to lead such a risky mission. No one boarded that wooden ship to sail into an unfamiliar ocean while leading a bunch of wily men simply because the data points looked good. (The data points looked horrendous.)

The same scenario holds true for you as a founder. Odds are low that you can convince superstar "captains" to join your mission. Your "ask" is a distinctly different process than asking a VC to invest their unemotional, well-diversified dollars.

Why? *Because the VC expects you to fail; your first employees do not.*

As such, design your recruitment "pitch" to understand an executive's values first (Who is that person sitting across from you?) and their skill set second.

Values are to be clearly defined in terms of what your company stands for and how you measure them. *Acting this way ensures the values of the people you hire fit your standard, consistently.*

Skill-set fit is about what skills the executive has to have today that will best serve your company's needs over the next several months (not years).

Tip #2—Recruiting Is Listening. Listening Is Learning. Learning Is Selling.

How you sell to these executives is based on listening for what is important to them through understanding *who they are* and *what they want.*

Remember to follow a high-touch, humanized approach. It is the mindset of benevolence that asks, "What is best for the person sitting across from me?"

Listen for it.

Ironically, you may discover you love their CV, but not them.

If you do feel a genuine connection, then feel free to share data from your pitch deck. Just make sure the facts and figures you share from your deck mirror what the executive you are recruiting cares about and is motivated by.

Stay on point—only highlight those items that matter to them.

As my friend Jay once told me, "Don't talk yourself out of the close." Invaluable advice for all of us.

Tip #3—Stop Sending LinkedIn Messages at Midnight (Better Yet, Don't Send Them After 5 p.m.)

Late-night, poorly crafted, generic pitches on LinkedIn, email, or text come across as a sloth-like, end-of-the-day thing, not a first-order priority that gets accomplished energetically during normal business hours.

"My team and I work round the clock. We have code to perfect, customers to delight, rent to pay, and investors to please. I know I have to recruit, but doing this after 5 p.m. is so much easier. It is the time I can step away from my other priorities and concentrate on recruiting."

Nice try.

With a lot of love, let's not accept your excuse.

You have reached this point in the book for a reason.

Be better. You want my help. Read on.

To be a great founder requires commitment to become an elite recruiter. I duly recognize you work long hours, and I feel the pressure you face every day.

Just hear me out.

If you put your recruiting hat on only at the end of an already intense day, potential hires will sense this. It won't be your best pitch. Low energy won't recruit the best talent. It is not a good practice to follow or to teach.

Prospects can sense droopiness. They can also sense too much caffeine. They want to sense another's posture, poise, and competence.

You are not going to put on a "recruiting hat." Recruiting should become your daily habit, not an article of clothing you take on and off.

The best founders embrace the grind. Their actions demonstrate that recruitment of top talent is a consistent daily practice, not an annoying chore to be done right before you doze off for the night.

"Understood. I need to make recruiting part of my routine, done at a time when I am energized not exhausted. What other tips do you have on how to message executives?"

Great question.

When energized, your messaging will naturally reflect this vibe: personalized, timely, and devoid of "stress," "rush," and "panic." These are the type of qualities we want others to associate with you.

As such, slow down and communicate with poise; don't use AI tools to message. Pepper messages with personal touches so the receiver knows it is you. Can you imagine explaining to your spouse that your love letter was written by a robot? Now think about how a star executive will feel if your handcrafted letter was not only written by an algorithm but also signed by it.

AI is a useful tool for a plethora of business challenges but be cautious on how you employ it when recruiting elite talent. We want dealings with you to be unique and feel meaningful (for everyone).

Be unique so dealings with you are meaningful (for everyone).

Often you won't get an immediate response. When this happens look at it as feedback and not defeat. For example, instead of saying, "The guy didn't return my call," maybe you should say, "If I'd left a more creative voicemail, maybe the guy would have called me back." Or, "If my voicemail had value and purpose, maybe the guy would have called me back."

> The reversal of blame toward others is not to blame yourself. Rather, it's to take responsibility for what happened, and create a lesson from it so that blame becomes responsibility, becomes an idea or a new strategy, and ultimately becomes a sale.
> —Jeffrey Gitomer

Gitomer is correct. Experiment, be creative, tweak how you message, and make it genuinely *you*. That's the kind of messaging that works. It gets attention.

Want an example? Enclose a handwritten note, in an overnight FedEx, to the office of the CTO commenting on her thoughtful YouTube presentation that you watched and enjoyed. In the note, leave your phone number and email and mention that you will call in a couple days to personally say "hello". Follow through and make that call. When she picks up your call invite her to coffee and let her recruitment begin.

It may seem like a big-time investment to personalize messages like this but ironically it will speed up hiring the right people. Star executives get bombarded all day with phony messaging devoid of originality.

Be energizing. Your enthusiasm will bring you the best. Because all of us are just waiting to feel alive and enthused again. We are all just waiting to hear from someone just like you.

Tip #4—Pick Up the Phone and Call

The core, fundamental reason you call is that no one calls anymore.

If you really want to stand out, pick up the phone and call.

Look, you had the guts to start a business. Is it that hard for someone as courageous as you to call?

Embrace "old school" practices. They work.

Before picking up the phone, close your eyes and remind yourself that your voice is an instrument (because it is). How you sound matters. What tone do you want to convey?

On that note (pun intended), I want you to follow Chris Voss's spot-on advice and speak with a late-night FM radio DJ voice:

> When I was teaching hostage negotiation, I knew a hostage negotiator might not even say the right things. If they had a great voice, we were probably going to be all right. Flipside, they could have all the techniques down. If they sounded like a robot, they were going to be horrible.
>
> —Chris Voss, former FBI hostage negotiator, speaker, and author

Here are some additional tactics to improve your game:

- If you get their voicemail, leave them an enthused audio message to simply call you back. Don't be wordy. If they don't call back within forty-eight hours, *call again.*
- Your voice message should be something like this: *Hi Jane, I have heard terrific things about you. What a stellar reputation you have. Let's chat. My name is _____ and against the wishes of most of my friends and family I founded a company,*

and thankfully it was the best decision I ever made. Let's chat more, I can't wait to hear more about you. Call me any time before 10 a.m. My number is (212) 122-8888. Again, that's (212) 122-8888."

EXPERT TIP: Always repeat your number twice even though it will automatically list on the receiver's cellphone. Some people still write things down, and you don't want them to have to replay your message to note your number correctly. Remove barriers; make it effortless to call you back.

EXPERT TIP: If a mutual friend referred you to this star executive, then mention said friend's name in your audio message. People almost always respond when there is a friend in common. For example, "Hi Jane, Pedro Rojas told me terrific things about you…"

- If after calling the prospect 2–3 different times and there is still no reply, then feel free to email/text.

By calling you show how interacting with you will be unique, efficient, and direct. Define boldness by practicing it.

Everyone knows this next statement to be true.

On a phone call you can perceive nuance and interpret tone exponentially better than when text messaging. As such, make calling your default medium when communicating with star executives. Don't be lazy and lob a text message. Doing so typically leads to misinterpretation and misunderstanding.

Pick up the phone and call.

Tip #5—Don't Play the Name Game

Remember that a person's name is to that person, the sweetest and most important sound in any language.
—Dale Carnegie

How many times does "Lynda" with a "y" get messages written "Linda"?

Be different. Lynda with a "y" will notice the one founder who spelled her name right.

Grammar, tone, and punctuation matter too. I cannot tell you how many people have errors on their LinkedIn accounts that would make my elementary teacher Mrs. Sheen groan. How we treat language matters.

Apply this same mindset to hiring.

Would you recommend hiring a CPA or an attorney who had punctuation errors on their LinkedIn profile?

I would not.

If you agree with me, then flip the script. Why would a star CPA come work for you if *your* LinkedIn profile and company web page is also sloppy?

The message is not to become a persnickety grammar teacher. The directive is to practice a standard in which your written communication reflects your company's culture for excellence.

Don't apologize for your commitment to this practice. Make it part of your startup's culture and watch how this often-overlooked tactic helps your company win the battle for top talent.

EXPERT TIP: Insist upon these same standards with incumbent members of your team. Have them double-check their LinkedIn profiles for grammatical correctness. Did they incorrectly capitalize "Director Of Facilities" versus "Director of

Facilities"? Also, insist that they take their time to spell others' names right. Set the standard company wide.

Tip #6—Stop Delegating to Your Junior Internal Recruiter

Simply put, star executives want to be recruited by the founder. Founders create an aura.

If you become the next Amazon, the star executives you are recruiting envision their future selves telling everyone at their MBA reunion how they were directly recruited by the new Bezos or Musk. They will prove how cool they are by showing everyone your number in their iPhone.

A founder who actively recruits sets the tone for the whole company. Want the best team? *Be the best example to follow.*

Need me to give you an inspirational nudge?

Cool. Internalize this succinct line from one of the best movies of all time:

Be the ball, Danny.
—Ty Webb (played by actor/comedian Chevy Chase in the movie *Caddyshack*)

Look, I am not against hiring an in-house recruiter. You will need help, especially as you grow. What I am recommending is to enroll in the belief that "more is caught than taught." Your junior recruiting person should shadow you, thereby learning what you want by observing you in action.

In the beginning phases of your startup, being hands-on in this way will prove more effective than trying to educate your team through emailed feedback, Zoom calls, or an all-hands training. Execute recruitment at this standard and let them see and hear you in action.

As you scale, delegate more and more to your HR Talent team. Through observation, they will have learned from you those essential elements of "soul" to be embedded in your internal recruitment processes. It does not mean you will stop recruiting, but as your company gets larger you can rely more on your team to manage the day-to-day process of recruitment.

However, from that initial business stage of 0 to 1, hiring the leadership team must be piloted by you.

Tip #7—Be Intentional with Round 2

How many times have I heard a founder say, "We had a great initial conversation and agreed to speak again next week."

When I ask, "What time/date next week did you schedule the second chat with the executive?" the founder inevitably responds, "Ah, I did not set a specific time/date yet."

Don't be that founder.

After an energizing first meeting with a star executive, call them and say this:

"What a terrific chat today. Let's open our calendars now and pick a good time for you to come back. How does next Tuesday at 8 a.m. sound to you?"

Pick the date and time that works for your calendars. It does not have to be Tuesday at 8 a.m. Thank you to the fantastic Chris Kearney, my old boss at Arthur Andersen, for teaching me this organizational technique. He asked this question countless times, and it worked flawlessly.

If the executive hesitates to book chat #2, they are typically not interested.

I can hear you now, grumbling and saying. . .

"But I just spent so much time and effort to meet this star executive. Do I just pack it in and move on because they made it hard to schedule chat #2?"

First, don't get frustrated if the star executive shows resistance to meeting again. Be calm, confident, measured—the opportunity to work with you and your team is not for everyone.

Next, hold back on your tendency to be relentless.

Relentlessness is one of the best traits a top founder can possess, but it can also be one of the worst. Your innate refusal to quit can get in the way when recruiting stars.

Instead, learn to recognize the quality of enthusiasm in others.

What this means is the executive you are recruiting has to reflect back at least a glimmer of enthusiasm for what you are trying to build. Otherwise, you risk pouring your "never give up" energy into recruiting an immovable wall. It ain't going to happen.

EXPERT TIP: Learn to let go if a star executive is not reciprocating enthusiasm or if this executive turns down your offer today. However, this does not mean you have to stop recruiting her. It may just be timing. The good news is if you treated her with authenticity and care, she will remember you in a positive way. If you still want to recruit her then call her 1–2 months after she said no. You may be surprised when she now enthusiastically says yes. If she still says no, then ask her who she recommends for the role. Good people hang out with good people, one of her friends may just be a perfect fit for your startup.

All right, let's step back and get to the point.

If you are having a hard time getting that star candidate on your calendar for second and third interviews, then don't chase. There exists a similarly qualified star candidate who will not only bring the technical chops to your startup but also an excitement to contribute.

Bottom line, focus your energy on those who return it.

When they do return it, then do not construct unnecessary barriers to having that second chat with them. Get this star candidate on your calendar right away. Capture the positive momentum.

It matters, especially when time is of the essence for your startup.

KEY TAKEAWAY

I've learned that people will forget what you said,
people will forget what you did, but people will
never forget how you made them feel.
—Maya Angelou

As a first-time founder, you quickly learn that to recruit
game-changers you have to become the best listener these
star executives have ever met. Being genuinely interested
in what's best for their career makes them feel valued.

Feeling valued is an emotional response, and the best
founders know that every decision people make is ultimately based on emotion (not logic).

By committing to a firmwide process where star executives feel listened to and understood, they will feel you
care, creating an environment of warmth and authenticity.
Also, by booking "on the spot" those second, third, and
fourth conversations, you create a flow of good energy and
positive momentum.

Combining this upbeat vibe with the action step of deliberate scheduling fosters positive emotion and increases the
odds that the star executive will ultimately accept your offer.

At the very least, your unique attention to the well-being of others becomes unforgettable. You become the type
of founder that game-changing executives cannot wait to
work for.

Isn't that the kind of founder you want to become?

Chapter 6

WHO BEFORE WHAT
THIS IS NOT YOUR
TEXTBOOK INTERVIEW

You never get a second chance to make
a first impression.
—*Oscar Wilde*

8:14 a.m.
Wednesday
Favorite Independent Coffee Shop

After following the "first contact" lessons, you did it. You
reached out to that star executive you never dreamed of
meeting, and she agreed to an in-person interview.

Lacking some glamorous office space with breathtaking views, you ask to meet near your coworking space at a local coffee shop.

You picked this spot intentionally. No loud music, the espresso is just right, and there's plenty of space to have an intimate conversation without distraction.

Ironically, you notice other first-time founders nearby who treasure this zenlike café to conduct important business.

In walks Jane Smith, the star CFO. You feel ready to make your first (and best) impression. You think you are you ready to interview, but how do you know?

That's where I come in.

It all starts with having a plan.

I can hear you sighing right now.

"How revolutionary. 'Have a plan.' Blah blah blah."

I know. It *is* boring, which is why most founders won't plan this initial conversation. "Winging it" is much more "fun" and "typical" compared to following a structured interview process.

However, it is that structure that not only keeps you focused on what is a "fit" but also creates a feeling of comfort for the interviewee.

Think about it. If most founders are going to simply "wing" it, when this star executive meets *you*, they'll feel a rare level of professionalism, creating an impression that working with you is something special.

Your process stands out. You'll come across as focused, serious, and dependable.

In short, do the boring plan to leave them with the critical impression that they can place their career in your hands.

"Fine—I'll plan for how I interview. Admittedly, by organizing a plan I'll also be less antsy. Feeling calmer will help me to better focus my energy on who fits my business, as well as create that 'trust' vibe with them. So how do I get started on the plan?"

To do it right, we're going to explore some critical first interview principles and practices. In total, these will help compose your plan.

Understand Who Before What

Do you start a first interview focused on the job description (e.g., the technical fit) *or* do you start each interview asking the candidate to share details about their personal lives?

To recruit at your best, start with *who*.

Who is the person sitting across from you? As my dear sister, Heather, taught me, everyone wants to share their story.

Be interested in it.

Explore their hobbies, family, life events, choices, and reasoning. Your curiosity will help you gauge their judgment.

Start with understanding "who" they are to uncover what motivates them and what they value. Pay attention.

Are their values aligned with the values of your startup? If no, then move on; it is not a fit. Be courteous and have a lighthearted chat about your business but don't keep interviewing when you know their values are clearly not aligned with yours.

If values feel aligned, then keep interviewing this executive to next understand the "what."

The "what" is what can be learned about their professional skills.

Do these skills fit what your startup needs over the next 1–5 months? Are these hard skills a strength of the candidate, an expertise? Or are these skills just something they have a superficial knowledge of and have never applied?

Once you have incorporated "who" and "what" as foundational elements into your interview process the next step is to zoom out.

The big picture of running an effective first interview is to maintain the mindset of "what is best for this person?" *before* "what does my company need?"

What your company needs comes second; who they are as a person comes first.

"That seems counterintuitive. Aren't I trying to understand what is best for my company? Also, I don't have time for this approach. I can't be having self-help sessions with candidates all day, listening to stories about how they got bullied in grade school and like to feed fire ants on the weekend."

Now hang on. You don't want to learn more about a star executive's fire ant collection? I think most of us would like to hear more about that one from a candidate!

All joking aside, let's address both of your concerns.

First, by nature of being a founder, your company and its interests are always top of mind. You would not have agreed to meet this person if their professional toolkit did not appear to apply to what your company needs help with now.

Second, you actually *save time* by having your first interview focused on understanding the person, not the CV.

Let's go your way and ignore their fire ant collection.

Instead of focusing on the person, you ask them technical questions that they ace. You fall in love with the glamour of their top 5 MBA, their startup experience, and their in-person charisma. You can already envision how easy fundraising will be with them on your team.

You set up more and more interviews with your team, and then they get interviewed by your board of directors. After weeks of interviews, someone on your board follows my counsel and digs into their values, motivators, and interests. This board member engages in a dialogue with a mindset of "What is best for this person sitting in front of me?"

Guess what happens next? By listening to learn, the board member decides that this sterling executive is not a cultural and values fit for your startup. They call you to say "not this person, no."

You just wasted everyone's time, including your own.

Let's go to extremes and imagine you politely veto your board member's opinion and hire this person anyway. You just cannot resist how good they are technically and figure you can manage their "questionable personality."

They start. After a month on the job, it is clear no one respects this person, they are not a cultural fit, and it is going to be mutiny if you don't ask them to leave.

All of this could have been avoided if you had simply laid the foundation of your interview process to be values-based first and technical second.

Truth be told, there is no silver bullet. However, by structuring your interview in a "who"-first way, you mitigate the risk of a bad hire.

At the risk of sounding like a broken record, I cannot stress enough the importance of the "who" part of your interview process. Let's revisit three gentle reminders on the topic before we move on to specific tactical interview techniques.

1. **Through people's personal stories we begin to understand the fabric of their lives.** These essential insights tell us about their values, who they listen to, and how they go about making decisions. It demonstrates their judgment.

2. **By showing genuine interest in their life stories, you diminish the fear of risk.** Many accomplished executives are fearful of joining a startup. This fear won't completely disappear, but when you listen to who they are with genuine care and curiosity you foster an *esprit de corps* that will make both

parties more inclined to embark upon this moon-shot, startup adventure together (or to decide not to).

3. **Conducting interviews that feel humane and less robotic creates an opportunity for authentic connection.** Look, people nowadays are used to staring at their cellphones for answers. They are not used to depth. They are not used to being "off script." They are not used to slowing down and having a real conversation. An interview where the focus is to calmly listen to their personal story versus cull instant data from their LinkedIn profile feels authentic to the interviewee. Authenticity fosters connection and connection leads to great hires.

As a founder, remind yourself constantly to connect.

Connection occurs when people feel listened to and understood. When people feel this way, they will like you. And when they like you, they are more likely to trust you and feel safe. Within this safe zone the executive will be more candid, honest, and vulnerable.

"Geez. If I hear that word 'vulnerable' one more time… Can you make this book a little less sappy?"

Yeah, I hear you. Let's be clinical and use the word "reciprocity." You listen to their treasured stories and share with them yours. Both of you are opening up to what matters to each of you.

My point is this: we want to create genuine connection through listening to ensure any potential working partnership is a good fit for both parties. To embark on this risky voyage, we want your initial interview to uncover a shared commitment. Can the two of you endure the inevitable ups and downs of startup life with humor, levity, teamwork, grace, and compassion (and, of course, results)?

Enough of the fluffy stuff. Let's get tactical.

Questions to Include When Interviewing

To begin, let's assume you have just raised your Series A funding round, your product is selling, and the books and records of your flourishing startup need better care. You no longer have time to organize all the financial projections, budgets, financial statements, and tax filings yourself. It's obvious to everyone—it's time to hire your first CFO.

Understanding Their Inner Circle of Influence

You have already learned the importance of going deep into a candidate's "who" side to build trust. Now ask these probing questions about their inner circle:

- Tell me about your close friends and family. Is anyone a CFO like you?
- How often do you and your family talk about work? If not your family, then who do you confide in when making big career decisions? Have they always agreed with you?
- Who knows you are meeting with me today? How did they react? Did anyone think it was too risky to join a startup?

(With this series of questions you gain insight into who they go to for advice, wisdom, and counsel. Also, you gain intel about how they go about making decisions which is invaluable information to understand as they consider joining your startup.)

If they have not told anyone in their inner circle about your startup, then ask, "Have you ever interviewed at a startup before?" If this *is* their first interview at a startup, then probe to better understand if the opportunity to be your CFO is of real interest or just them being curious. (Enthusiasm is better than curiosity.)

Understanding Personality and Motivation

Now that you've gotten a sense of who they listen to and confide in, it's time to incorporate questions that uncover insights into their personality and motivators. These will help you comprehend what they really value, what triggers frustration, and what moves them to take action.

- Tell me about the day you first became a CFO. Was your promotion unexpected? Why did the promotion not happen sooner?

(Here we gain insight into what they did to become a CFO [*Did they earn it?*] and the timeline of their promotion [*Are they frustrated/show defensiveness that their promotion took too long?*])

- Who is the best CFO you know? What makes her the best? What do you wish she did differently?

(Here we gain insight into how they view a successful CFO. We also learn how this role model CFO could indirectly influence decisions at your startup. By asking what their role model should do differently, we learn more about the candidate's self-confidence, coachability, judgment, and attachment.)

- Tell me about your best friend—when and where did you meet? What does he do for work? Did he always think you would be a CFO? If not, what would he tell me you should be doing with your talent? In other words, how would your best friend describe your ideal career/dream life ten years from now?

(Here we gain insight into how a very important person in

this CFO's life defines fulfillment for them. Ideally, this friend knew the candidate before university and the job market. *Since personality tends to be static, we get an unadulterated, "childhood" view of who the candidate is and their motivators.*)

- Do you know someone who has a really good job but in reality is avoiding doing what they should be doing with their time, talent, and energy? They do good work, but something is holding them back from pursuing their true calling. From your heart, what's really going on? What is holding this person back?

Listen to their response then ask the critically important second part of the question:

- Now, imagine I asked this person the same question about you. If they were here with us now, would they tell me that you are delighted to be a CFO? Or could they convince us a different role would be more fulfilling for you?

(Similar to the best friend question above, this series of questions provides insight into how this member of their inner circle feels about their career choices. Note the order of the questions. *We intentionally ask them to critique this trusted person first.* Once they critique this other person it will be easier for them to critique themselves.)

- Tell me about your last vacation. Tell me about your next one. When vacationing, how would your staff describe their interaction with you?

(Here we gain insight into how they balance work and rest.

As much as startups want someone to be working tirelessly on building the company, it is critical that your team has routines for stepping away from work. Seeing how they plan for future vacations is just as important as them having taken past vacations. It demonstrates a routine for maintaining balance, a life outside of the office, and mental health. It can also demonstrate how they organize their team and delegate so that their function runs efficiently, even when they are on vacation.)

KEY TAKEAWAY

Insightful questions help to uncover who is really sitting across from you. The focus is not so much on what the candidate tells us about themselves but rather how others view them, who they confide in, and actions they have taken. (*Is there a pattern?*) As Sigmund Freud so eloquently stated, "The *you* that you know is hardly worth knowing."

By asking questions that reveal *others' opinions* of this CFO, you capture a more accurate picture of how they are in their day-to-day work. Simply stated, how others view them is their reputation.

And don't you want a reputation for hiring the best?

Chapter 7
A STAR IS BORN
HOW TO ASSESS CAPABILITY

"OK, Patrick, you have convinced me I need to know the 'who' before the 'what.' Also, I feel much better having example questions that will uncover their personality, drivers, and motivators. But how do I figure out in an interview if they actually know what they are doing? I don't want to hire a person who has great values but cannot deliver exceptional work."

Bingo! You must avoid the charlatans. To do so, focus on these three areas to feel confident that this executive can excel at the work you are asking them to do:

1. Attitude
2. Aptitude
3. Judgment

Attitude

Attitude is a little thing that makes a big difference.
—Winston Churchill

When interviewing executives remind yourself that attitude is their motor; it powers an enthusiasm to own the tasks they are assigned. *The right attitude brings a bias for action.* They are not afraid to make a call even when they don't have all the data. It's not recklessness, just good judgment + positive intent used decisively. The right attitude is conscientious of timing, preferring to act quickly rather than stand still and allow the window of game-changing opportunity to close.

In startup world, the right attitude makes a move. Moreover, the right attitude never thinks of it as "*your* startup." Instead, the right executive has what all startup founders crave: they think, work, and *act* like an owner. They take decisions personally, as if they were the founder.

"The framework makes sense. It reminds me of Jocko Willink's concept of extreme ownership—taking responsibility for everything in your world. But what exactly should I ask in the interview to recognize the traits of agility, action, and accountability? Examples, please!"

You got it! But first, can you imagine interviewing Jocko to run operations at your startup? He would love to answer the questions I am about to share.

Determining an Executive's Attitude
Before questioning an executive about their attitude, first-time founders need to get into the right mindset.

Breathe, slow down, and be mindful for the signals of "Does this executive have the attitude of an owner?" The right mindset attunes you to better perceive the presence of owner like traits.

For example, owners are prepared. They also take personal responsibility for failures and credit others when successful. They "play well with others." They also think outside their job description, problem-solve, and act consistently in the best interest of the company.

As soon as you feel calm, primed, and present to feel for these ownership characteristics, you are ready to ask the following interview questions:

1. When was the last time you and your boss debated a decision? How did you resolve it?
   - Look for preparation, "big picture" thinking, trustworthiness, and teamwork.
   - If they have never debated with their boss, then ask about debates with a peer, customer, or staff member.

2. What is the best way for your current employer to grow now? Over the next 2–3 years? Why has that not happened yet?
   - Look for strategic thinking, accountability, product/market knowledge, and humility.

3. What project did you act on or participate in that was outside your job description/expertise? What was the outcome? What could have been done differently to get better results?
   - Look for initiative, teamwork, preparation, resourcefulness, bias to act, agility, and results.

4. When was the last time you faced uncertainty at work? What happened next?

• Look for bias for action, judgment, creativity, collaboration, and accountability.

5. What is the worst thing your boss would tell me about you?
  • Look for humility, self-awareness, narcissism, and self-improvement.

By including these questions in your interview process, you'll learn about the attitude of the executive sitting before you. Gauging this specific capability provides reassurance that they possess "grit"—an essential ingredient to thrive in the roller-coaster environment of startup jobs.

"In summary, you want me to be present. Mentally ready to receive evidence that they have the right attitude for the startup world. Once primed, I can then ask the questions above. Makes sense, but I still don't have any questions to determine their technical skill set. How do I test for that?"

You're exactly right. First, you must be primed and ready to understand an executive's attitude. They can have all the technical gifts in the world, but if they're a jerk it isn't going to work.

Aptitude

When interviewing for aptitude, companies will often test for evidence of technical skill. For a CTO, they might observe the quality of their code base in action. For a CFO, they might ask for a walkthrough of their method for budgeting and forecasting. Technical questions and other more traditional methods[4] for assessing an executive's "hard" skills should be part of any first-time founder's interview process. However, when interviewing for the right *startup profile* **you need more than this traditional approach.** Not only must you interview for technical skill (can they make an apple pie?) but also for an executive's learning approach (how would they make an apple pie without the apples?).

"How in the heck do I do that? And what in the world is 'learning approach'?"

Perhaps the best way to illustrate the point is through an interview question posed by the inventor of Amazon Prime, who asked job applicants, *"What is your strategy for learning?"* The power of the question resides in its ability to draw out tangible examples of how the executive sitting before you learns.

After asking this question yourself, sit back, and listen for examples of projects, overcoming obstacles, and teamwork. As the dialogue unfolds stay attentive to the following questions:

- *How do they go about problem-solving? Who taught them and how was it taught?*
- *When has their knowledge base and/or traditional problem-solving method failed to solve an issue? What happened next?*

---

4 Traditional ways to test technical ability include utilizing case studies, conducting a trusted technical expert interview and commenting on the executive's technical chops, reference checking focused on technical knowledge, and even scheduling a test drive of the candidate (i.e., working on a thirty-day project at your business before formalizing an official offer). The best way to verify technical competence is the "test drive" method but rarely is it practical to ask a full-time employee to leave their current employer without a guarantee of a full-time offer from you.

- *What actions do they take to stay current in their area of expertise? How often?*
- *What actions do they take to stay informed from a macro sense? In other words, how do they learn outside of their expertise? How often?*
- *What belief do they hold today that they did not hold in the recent past? Look for strong opinions, loosely held. It signals flexible thinking, agility, teamwork, and humility.*

These insights help you to discover if the executive you are interviewing values growth, practices continuous learning, and is open-minded—all fundamental elements of a healthy learning style well-suited for your startup environment.

"Other than testing for hard technical skills and inquiring to understand their learning approach, are there other recommended attributes to be on the lookout for? I want to do all I can to ensure this executive has the aptitude for my startup."

Yes. Let's explore four I highly recommend.

Fast Learner

As mentioned, understanding an executive's strategy for learning is of the utmost importance when hiring for your startup. But go even deeper. Focus on how fast they can learn something new, something they have never seen before.

In any startup, unforeseen challenges will inevitably arise. Use this series of questions to grade how quickly the executive will react, learn, and adapt:

- Was there ever a problem at work that you had never encountered before?
- How did you go about recognizing the problem?
- What happened next?

Most executives can identify problems—that is table stakes. We want more. Does this executive show how they quickly adapted to resolve the problem? What was the timeline? Did the problem ever get resolved? What did it cost?

Look for adeptness, a bias for action and results, curiosity, succinct presentation, and an awareness of budget. (It's a bonus if the executive being evaluated is also conscientious of dollars and cents; often startups must do more with less since they lack the financial resources of established companies.)

Remember, the core of the questioning is to measure how fast they adapted to resolve unexpected problems. Not only will you get a sense of the velocity of their problem-solving skills, but you also get insight into the next essential attribute: intellectual curiosity.

Intellectual Curiosity

Ever met someone who was set in their ways? How did that feel? One thing we know about building a startup is that what works today may not work tomorrow. Your customers' preferences may change overnight. How your team adapts, pivots, and grows through change matters. As such, hiring for the trait of intellectual curiosity profoundly improves the odds your company will grow (and survive). Ask these questions to uncover its existence:

- What one thing about our product or company do you like? And what would you change?

As they respond, you will get a sense of their curious nature (or lack thereof). Keep more of a focus on what they would change by probing further with the follow-up question "Tell me more." Then ask, "How did you come to that conclusion?"

As a founder, understanding how they view your company and how they would change it reveals not just their curiosity but also their logic, reasoning, preparedness, and strategic vision.

• Are you self-taught in any skills?

This question offers all kinds of avenues for you, as the founder, to explore how, why, what, and when they learn. As you are listening, probe further by focusing on their process, their time commitment, and their level of mastery. Also, feel out the degree of their natural curiosity. How deep do they go? Is their level of depth a fit for your company's values?

• Tell me about a side project you have done outside of work. What motivated you to do it? What did you learn along the way that surprised you? How long did you work on it? Did you stop? If yes, what was the real reason you stopped? It's OK to tell it to me straight; no one wants the textbook answer.

Here we're looking for an inquisitive nature, motivators, a self-improvement attitude, and commitment.

Understand why, when, and how they may have quit a project. *Quitting is critical to understand.* Do they lose focus because they are overly inquisitive and get bored easily? Is there a tendency to move on to the next shiny thing before finishing a routine task?

EXPERT TIP: First-time founders should look for signs of intellectual curiosity but also for commitment and perseverance. Although startups have glamorous projects and lofty goals, there is still a lot of routine "grunt" work that must be done. Executives who are too focused on the next big thing and not willing to roll up their sleeves to see a worthwhile project through to completion typically won't be a good fit for your startup team.

Teamwork

Assessing an executive's teamwork capability through an in-person interview is really hard. It would be much easier to assess through a short-term project conducted with you and members of your team, but this is rarely practical. Most executives will not commit to the proverbial "test drive" before joining your startup.

Accordingly, ask the following questions to get a sense of their teamwork skills:

- Tell me about the last project you and your team did that was a spectacular success.
- Now tell me about that one project that was a total nightmare.

We want the focus to be on the nightmare project. We ask for the positive example first because when you start with their winning project you create an environment of likeability and safety. It allows the interviewee to be more vulnerable, open, and trusting when sharing their nightmare project story.

Within the nightmare story, look for defensiveness, blaming others, narcissism, lack of resourcefulness, learning lethargically, no pivoting, no metrics, disorganization, team turnover, and bad communication.

But also look for positives such as overcoming obstacles,

cohesion, humility, collaboration, and trust. According to Google's research on high-functioning teams, the most important factor in a team's success was psychological safety. In other words, within strong teams no one is afraid to look dumb for making a mistake, offering their opinion, or challenging an assumption.

- Who was the best boss you ever worked for?
  Who was the worst?

Listen for the attributes of their role-model boss. Does this description fit how others would describe your management style? Your culture? Be brutally self-aware. Are you this type of leader now?

Equally, pay attention to the defects of their worst boss. How does this description gel with your culture? How does it compare to how others would describe you as a boss?

- Does anyone at your company know you are interviewing with me today?
- If you decided to leave your company and join us, would your co-workers be surprised? Tell me more.

Look for signs of high or low trust among the executive's co-workers. Does their answer feel gossipy? If yes, is that the kind of leader you want on your team?

The importance of teamwork is self-explanatory. Use the tactical questions above to assess if the executive before you will enhance or diminish your startup's effectiveness as it relates to "team." Once you get a sense of their teamwork capability, then move on to the last essential element of aptitude.

Selling Skills

I don't care if you are a technical founder.
You are selling. Every founder is a salesperson.
—Parker Treacy, co-founder of Cobli.

Parker is right. As a first-time founder, your sales skills are essential to your startup's survival and success. If you are:

- unable to persuade the customer to buy—**Out of business.**
- unable to convince investors to invest—**Out of business.**
- unable to recruit and run a high-functioning team—
  Out of business.

Yet, it is not just founders who need selling skills. Your leadership team should also possess this aptitude.

"Makes sense. But how do I interview for selling skills?"

First, ignore the infamous "sell me this pen" scene from the movie *The Wolf of Wall Street*. We don't want schtick or gimmicks. We want trustworthiness coupled with persistence, listening, and connection. To understand if the executive sitting across from you has these qualities, ask these questions:

- If I handed you a piece of paper and a pen, how would you describe yourself to someone who has never met you in a simple, one-page outline.

Listen to how they tell their story. How are they outlining their life? Do you feel a connection? Trust? Did they follow directions and keep it succinct, or are they rambling? Would you buy from them? Would your clients? Do they show curiosity? Creativity? Are they engaging with you and the question?

- Ever really want to hire someone and they said no? Tell me more. What happened next?

The goal is to understand their attitude and response to rejection. Look for resourcefulness, persistence, follow-up, curiosity, self-awareness, and resilience.

If they have *never* been responsible for hiring someone then ask:

- When was the last time you went after something and it did *not happen* (e.g., applied for a top MBA and got rejected, interviewed somewhere and did not get the job, or didn't receive a promised promotion or requested transfer)? Tell me more, what happened next?

Look for blaming others and excuses but also resourcefulness, persistence, follow-up, curiosity, self-awareness, and resilience.

Selling skills begin and end with the person having an aura of trust. As the executive answers the questions above, are you feeling that tingle of trust? Do they come across as someone you, your team, your investors, and your customers would feel is credible?

Remember, sales skills can be learned—how to connect, how to listen, how to use your voice like an instrument, how to tell a story, how to sell to SMBs, how to use metrics, etc. *However,* hiring an executive who lacks a foundation of believability will negatively impact your startup.

It is mutual trust, even more than mutual interest,
that holds human associations together.
—H. L. Mencken

Simply stated, Aptitude is much more than a technical test. To focus only on a candidate's "hard skills" runs the risk of hiring a technical genius who is a total jerk or the know-it-all who does not listen. This personality type is not going to help your startup thrive.

Instead, follow the holistic approach to measure aptitude as outlined above. In this way you will gain insight into their natural curiosity and agility and whether they have the ability to work well with others. You will also get a feel for whether they have an engaging listening style and, most importantly, whether they seem dependable, reliable, and trustworthy.

In the end, don't we all want to work with people we trust?

Judgment

> Good judgment is the result of experience and
> experience the result of bad judgment.
> —Mark Twain

Earlier in discussing aptitude, we learned why it is important as a first-time founder to understand how the executive sitting before you learns. But how does learning apply to judgment?

How an executive applies what she has learned from previous experience is their judgment. As Mark Twain observed a century ago, we want to hire someone who has developed good judgment through all the various learnings they have experienced. In particular, founders should be laser-focused on understanding how the executive candidate has dealt with mistakes, taken responsibility for actions, and improved their judgment as a result.

Here are three concrete methods to know whether (or not) the executive you are interviewing has the self-awareness and learning approach to foster good judgment.

Test Drive Project

A good old-fashioned test drive is the most reliable way to understand any executive's judgment. Simply create a short-term project at your startup in which you can see the executive in action and accompany the "how and when" in their decision-making.

However, as my counsel on aptitude showed, it is rarely possible that a full-time executive will leave their job to work on a three-month project for your startup without a guarantee of a full-time offer.

If the test-drive option is not viable then consider a case study that models what you are looking to hire. If neither of these approaches are doable then employ the second-best method to test judgment: the reference check.

Reference Check

In a reference check, you will want to speak to their former boss, a peer, *and* a staff member they supervised. Also, an outside client/customer if possible. With these people ask the following:

- Tell me about a project that "John Smith" worked on that exemplified his work product.
- During this project, what decisions did John have sole responsibility for?
- Of those particular decisions, which one was good but not great?
- What would have made it great?
- If John were here with us now, would he strongly agree with you?

The difference between "good" and "great" is subtle but intentional. The person responding to your reference check may not want to tell you about how John made bad decisions (if they do, listen attentively).

However, they should share how John's good decision could have been better. In this way, we get the person giving the reference to be more open and detailed about the depth of John's judgment.

Discovering how John makes decisions, as well as his openness to others' feedback, is the intent of the questions above. In conducting the reference check, was John consistently flexible or defensive? Was he listening? Aware of biases? Overconfident? Adaptive?

Look for coachability, self-awareness, recognition of mistakes, and humility. According to Dr. Robert Hogan, co-founder of the famed Hogan Assessment, people's decisions plus how they react to feedback create their reputation for judgment. Furthermore, Dr. Hogan believes that good judgment involves a willingness to fix bad decisions and learn from experience.

Next, look for signs of *how* John made decisions. Was he more data-driven or did he employ a "gut instinct" and "shoot from the hip" approach? Was he more interested in form than function when making decisions?

As you listen, evaluate the various references' responses. Are you comfortable that there is alignment with the kind of judgment your startup needs from this executive?

If not, don't hire John Smith.

Career History

Here we want to focus on the decisions made from accepting their first job offer through to joining their current job. As a first-time founder, it is particularly attractive if during their job moves they have taken less money at a company because they wanted to improve themselves. Typically, a decision like this shows enjoyment of continuous learning and that elusive growth mindset—highly desirable traits of a successful startup executive.

When conducting these questions around the executive's career history, do not let them drive the dialogue, as it is something most executives have practiced numerous times in an interview setting. *Instead, get them "off script" by making them follow your lead and pace.* To do so, inform the interviewee that you will ask some questions about their career path and, from time to time, you may interrupt just to stay on topic. Then, ask these specific questions to better understand their judgment skill:

- At the time you were graduating college, which companies did you interview at?
- Did you get offers from all the companies you interviewed? If not, what company would you have joined if you had received an offer?
- Tell me more.

EXPERT TIP: "Tell me more" is that simple phrase that opens up all kinds of interesting information about the executive sitting before you. Ask it, then sit back and let it work its magic.

If they received offers from every company they interviewed at then ask:

- What was it about Company X that made you join them rather than accept Company Y's offer? What was Company Y missing? Knowing what you know now, would you make that same decision?
- Tell me more.
- Was there anywhere you really wanted to work but did not get an interview?

If yes, then probe to see if where they wanted to interview back in the day is aligned with where they work today. If not, then try to understand what changed. Do they feel regret?

We are seeking to understand how they learn, make decisions, and act as a basis for assessing their judgment. Next add:

• Thank you. Would you now briefly walk me through why you moved from your first job to the job you have today.

Remember, take the lead and ensure they are succinct. If they are verbose, it can signal a lack of "bias for action," which typically won't fit in the environment of early-stage startups.

Be attuned to their decision-making, who recruited them, and what motivated them to change. Look for poise, rationality, and consistency in their judgment.

As they talk about their job history, here are the four key themes to understand:

1. *Money:* How often did making more money drive their job moves? Did they ever take a new job for less money? Why? Would they do that again?

2. *Losing a Job:* did they ever get downsized or terminated? What happened? Are they succinct in their explanation? Bitter and blameful?

3. *Recruitment:* Did their former colleague/boss recruit them for a new job? More than once? Usually, it is a positive sign of competence and teamwork skills when former bosses/colleagues invite an executive to join them again (and again) at a new company.

4. Counteroffer: Did they ever receive a counteroffer to stay at an employer? Did they accept it? Have they taken a counteroffer more than once? Would they consider a counteroffer again? What did they learn from taking a counteroffer?

Once you have surveyed their career history, it's time to understand the here and now. Ask this last question to close the loop on how they manage their career decisions:

• If I asked your closest friends/inner circle, what would they agree is the truth, the real reason you are leaving your current job?

This question seems standard, but it's slightly atypical of what most people expect.

Don't ask, "Why are you looking to leave your job?" Instead, ask the question recommended here to uncover a) what other people would say is this executive's actual motivation to change jobs and b) to assume that they "are leaving." Don't ask if they are *open to leave*—be confident and direct in assuming they are leaving their current job.

Why?

First, *we want the perspective of their inner circle.* The consistency of how others see this executive more accurately predicts their motives and actions. The viewpoint of others gives us insight into this executive's true judgment.

Second, *we want to plant the seed that by sitting with you to chat about your startup they are leaving their current job.* If the executive does not correct this assumption, you just confirmed their openness to leave for the right opportunity.

Sometimes, the executive will correct you and say they are

not looking to leave. If this is the case, don't invest too much time trying to motivate an unenthusiastic executive.

> Motivation is simple. You eliminate
> those who are not motivated.
> —Lou Holtz

Coach Lou cuts to the chase and reminds you to keep it simple. Look for those who will join your startup with genuine enthusiasm for what you are trying to build. Without that vibe, they won't be a good hire.

EXPERT TIP: Dig deeper to understand their motivation to change by asking the following: "Do you remember that actual day when you just knew you were not going to stay long-term at the company? Tell me more about what happened that day, in that meeting, at that moment." Getting a detailed example gives insight into their judgment and can help you close this executive at the time of an offer. When making your offer you will remind them of this tangible issue and how it inspired them to interview with you in the first place. Moreover, you will assure them that this problematic issue is a thing of the past. It won't happen at your startup.

> The most impactful decisions in a business are usually the
> ones that are made under uncertainty.
> —Andy Rachleff, inventor of the term "product/market fit"
> and Benchmark Capital venture investing legend

Rachleff is correct. In trying to achieve greatness at your startup you will constantly run into uncertainty. By implementing the shared techniques, first-time founders can build teams who are better prepared to address and resolve ambiguity. In the end, these founders are advised by teams who bring good judgment. With good judgment, they increase the probability of better decision-making.

In short, when a first-time founder gets hit with the inevitable "what do we do now?" he will be elated that he hired executives whose judgment along with their enthusiasm and aptitude are up to the task.

KEY TAKEAWAY

Assessing another's ability is best done through direct observation. But rarely will you get the chance to "test drive" a star executive before they start working full-time at your startup. As such, utilize the techniques outlined to gain a vital glimpse of how they think, speak, and act, to vastly improve your judgment of whether they're the right team addition or it's best to keep looking. One's capability should not be left to chance.

Chapter 8
CLINCH THE CLOSE

Begin by always expecting good things to happen.
—Tom Hopkins

ey founder, great job!

You now possess core lessons to attract and evaluate top talent far beyond those founders who have not done their elite recruiting homework. Let them wing it; you are going to crush it.

You've learned that interviewing is about the *other* person; *listening* is selling.

You know how to focus on a person's values, understand their inner circle of influence, and assess if the executive you are recruiting can "walk the talk."

Ready to put it all together?

It's time to talk about closing.

Being a prepared founder who expects good things to happen is one thing. Being an unprepared founder who hopes for the best when recruiting star executives is another. Because the old cliché rings true. Hope is not a strategy . . . and therein lies the problem. How many founders do you know who have heartbreaking stories of the candidate that, at the last minute, changed their mind?

They could not close the deal.

Or worse, the candidate who kept delaying his start date, until suddenly, after three months of making the founder wait, said, "No thank you" accompanied by the classic nonsensical line, "I would love to join you, but I have not yet finished my cycle."

To become a "closer" it is not about having hope, cranking out charming lines, or sending a basket of gifts to a star executive's home.

To close well, you have to be "boring."

When I say "boring," I'm not referring to dull. It means being prepared, asking direct questions, and doing this over and over consistently. You can send the champagne *after* the star executive accepts.

To be a "closer," follow the steps I lay out below. This is your "boring" plan.

It is a continuation of what I have been outlining since we started: be curious, ask pointed questions, and maintain focus on what is best for the elite executive you are interviewing. From that foundation you will close star executives quickly and gracefully.

"Got it. Can we begin with your tips already?"

Easy, Cowboy.

To begin, let's introduce the two most important words in the English language for ensuring your offers are accepted: *trial closing*.

The Art of Trial Closing

Relax, no one is going to jail. It is not that kind of trial. Goodness, I hope I am not teaching you how to recruit for a criminal enterprise!

I digress.

"Please stop with the dad jokes. I realize this is not prepping me for law school or to be a litigator. What is trial closing?"

Fine. Pause has been pressed on the dad jokes.

Trial closing is a series of intentionally provocative questions. They are direct, almost blunt in nature, and asked with positive intent.

What these questions are meant to do is "cut the crap" with candidates. Use them to save a lot of time and avoid unnecessary heartache. When done correctly, a good trial close makes the entire offer/acceptance process *uneventful*.

"What does 'uneventful' mean?"

It means that there is no "closing drama" where you make an offer and then have to anxiously await their inevitable "no."

Instead, you identified the right executive, relevant details were discussed, the executive is in agreement, they sign the offer letter, and *voila*, they start. Simple.

But, before we dive into the questions, know that a proper trial close begins by *establishing connection*.

Establishing Connection

Be brutally honest with yourself—who is the person at your company that everyone loves? Is it you or is there another co-founder or founding team member who just has "it" with people?

If the natural "connector" is not you, accept it; ego cannot get in the way of hiring the best.

To trial close effectively, quickly identify which member of your team the star executive feels most comfortable confiding in, sharing concerns with, and revealing their genuine motivations to change jobs.

Do not assume you know who it is.

Instead, when chatting with the executive you are interviewing, inquire in a humble, easygoing tone the following:

- Everyone here is excited about you and your work. Their experience with you has been so positive. What I am curious about is how *you* are feeling and what, so far, has been good for *you*. Of everyone you have met, who has been easiest to talk to? Who do you feel you connected with the most?

Through observation and by asking for your team's feedback, it should be obvious who this executive "clicks" with. *But ask the above to verify your hunch.* Remember, don't assume you know.

EXPERT TIP: For the interviewee, this question can be uncomfortable, as they may be hesitant to share that they connect better with someone other than you. As such, consider having your HR leader ask the question or, if you have hired a headhunter, instruct the headhunter to ask the interviewee who she feels is the most *credible* person at your startup.

You cannot fake chemistry. And remember, when people like each other they tend to trust each other.

So, find out who has the trust of the star executive candidate you are recruiting and ensure they are involved in the trial closing. This team member should also be available to assist with onboarding and play defense against the inevitable counteroffer (which we'll cover in chapter 11).

"Okay, I need to find out who has the best connection with the star executive to increase the probability that they will join my startup. Once it is determined who 'clicks' with this executive I will involve them in the interview process. Understood. But what next?"

The next step is asking those pesky yet highly effective trial close questions. Let's dive in.

Direct Questions Get Direct Answers

Here we want to ask those precise, laser-beam questions to ensure a smooth offer/acceptance process. Some questions may feel awkward but remember that they serve to surface concerns that can get in the way of the star executive accepting your offer.

Each of these questions is related to a theme. So let's list the five most common themes and their related trial close questions:

Theme #1: The Opportunity Itself

After each interview you will want to gauge the executive's actual interest level to join your startup. For an example, let's assume we are recruiting the star executive "Jane Smith." At the end of each interview, ask Jane the following:

• Jane, I wanted to quickly call to ask about your interview today. How are you feeling? What did you learn about us that you liked? Any concerns?

Again, throughout the entire interview process you will want to ask a variant of the above question. Obviously, you don't want to repeat this question verbatim seven times in a row, or you will sound like a robot.

Instead, mix it up; phrase the question in different ways to know what Jane liked and disliked about the opportunity itself. Understanding what she cares about provides essential data for future conversations. And understanding her concerns helps you to resolve objections *before* you make a formal offer.

EXPERT TIP: Always call the executive for feedback or ask for it in person. Getting their feedback via text messaging is not recommended. Remember my earlier advice to "pick up the phone."

Theme #2 - Team Chemistry
Similar to asking Jane at the end of each interview what she liked or did not like, you should also ask a variation of the following question throughout her interview process:

- Jane, how are you feeling about our team? Would you work well with everyone? Or is there anyone here you feel might be harder to work with? Who has been your favorite team member so far?

Like my comments on establishing connection, does Jane see herself "clicking" and collaborating with you and your founding team? We want chemistry, synchronicity.

Remember to keep your radar up to detect who she likes the most. That person is going to help you close Jane to join your startup.

Also, be on the lookout for a team member she just cannot work with. What can you learn from that feedback? Is that a dealbreaker, or can you work it out?

Theme #3 – Other Activity

Don't be naïve. Star candidates like Jane always have numerous suitors. If you are truly recruiting an elite executive, be surprised if they *don't* have various employers pursuing them.

To know where you stand, get in the habit of asking versions of the following question during post-interview chats:

• Jane, it seems things are really going well; we had another great chat with you today. Outside of your interviews with us, do you have any other interviews, offers, or internal things at work that you are considering?

Continuously ask this question or get blindsided when Jane tells you after five rounds of interviews at your startup, dinner with your founding team, etc. that she has decided to stop interviewing with you and move to Sydney because the internal transfer she was waiting for finally came through.

EXPERT TIP: If Jane does have interview activity with other companies, are these other companies startups? If not, and her other interviews are at big, stable firms, she may be wasting your time. Typically, a star executive interested in your startup will want to compare you to other startups, not risk-averse, traditional companies.

Theme #4 - Money

Never leave the conversation about money for the end of your recruitment process. Doing so is a *classic error* that violates the principles of a good trial close.

One of the key moments to understand money with a star executive is during the first interview when they are walking you through their job history.

Job History

To best illustrate the concept, let's return to "Jane Smith" as our example executive.

As part of any formal interview, you will want to understand why Jane left one job to take another. This technique is Interviewing 101.

But, as a first-time founder, you want to dig deeper. Be curious. *What is her motto about money?*

As she walks you through her past to present jobs keep asking:

- What was your last salary at the old job compared to the starting salary at the new job? Any bonus or stock plan?

Listen intently for clues about the following:

- *Did Jane ever take less money to gain a new skill?*
- *Does Jane seem to focus on cash or equity?*
- *Is there a trend to how she thinks about wealth? Is it consistent with her actions?*
- *Did Jane ever turn down an offer because, at the time, the salary was too low?*
- *Did she regret that decision later on? If yes, why?*
- *Did she accept a counteroffer?*
- *How did Jane go about making the decision to join each new company? Is there a pattern? Is she money motivated?*
- *Does she take weeks to accept an offer or does she accept quickly, resign from the old job, and start right away at the new job? How does she go about making decisions?*

By being attuned to how she thinks about money and makes decisions, you learn how to customize your formal offer in a way that appeals to how Jane has acted in the past.

EXPERT TIP: When getting details about her salary (and cash and stock bonuses), take note of the calendar date of her last raise and the calendar dates of her next cash and stock bonuses/vesting schedule. The timing of these cash-related items can affect her start date and how she negotiates an offer with you. Bottom line: Knowing the dates of these compensation items matter, so ask about them.

In addition to understanding money matters through her job history, the money topic should also be explored in the context of Jane's personal life.

Personal Life

Losses loom larger than gains.
—Amos Tversky and Daniel Kahneman

For many people, the pain of losing $100 is greater than the joy of winning $200.

If Jane is loss-averse, then it is better to move on. She is not going to accept your offer because startups are too risky for her. She is "window shopping."

"*Whoa.* Don't be so judgmental. Maybe Jane needs time to understand how our compensation plan could work for her. Is there a way to really know if she is window shopping?"

Okay, let me slow it down (a bit).

To separate the window shoppers from those committed to startups, it is important to understand how their personal lives influence their decision-making.

To gain this clarity, ask Jane the following:

- Tell me more about your family and friends. Have you told any of them you are meeting me and my startup team?
- For those that you trust, how would you convince them that joining a startup is a no-brainer?

Listen, then to *really* make these questions work their magic say, "Tell me more."

These questions deliver invaluable insights into her personal preferences for risk-taking and money. Listen for and be curious about the following:

- *Is there financial pressure at home that would preclude her from joining your risky startup?*
- *Is there a reason she did not tell anyone she is interviewing at your startup? If she did tell people, were they excited for her?*
- *Does Jane have family and friends who are at startups? Do they love it, or are they filled with regret?*
- *Did any of her inner circle become fabulously wealthy by taking risks? If yes, what counsel would they give her about your startup?*

Embedded in her personal life, as well as her job history, are consistent actions that tell you, the first-time founder, how she feels about taking risks and making money. I cannot stress enough how important it is to understand her relationship with these topics early on in the interview process. The questions above open the door to understanding. They normalize a sensitive topic.

What you gain in this approach is obvious.

If you discover that Jane is not a risk-taker and her fear about money is greater than the upside your startup can provide, then you saved a lot of time. You did not have to suffer a declined offer or additional wasted hours of interviewing, board approvals, and reference checking.

In reality, most people like the comfort of cash now versus the future wealth potential of stock options; don't take it personally and move on from executives who are too traditional in this regard.

On the flipside, if she is open to the risk at your startup, you have now normalized the touchy topic of compensation.

"That makes a lot of sense. Waiting until the end of the interview process to talk about money is bad strategy. From the beginning of my chats with 'Jane,' I will be attuned to her relationship with money by paying attention to details in her professional and personal life. Let's go with the assumption that through her interview I am comfortable she is open to risk and is enthused about joining my startup. What do I do next?"

Now is the time to talk to Jane about a *hypothetical offer.* Begin with the following:

Jane, it seems we are both excited about working together and we also see money in a similar way. As you can imagine, I have to be sensitive to cash flow, budget, the team, our investors, and the board with regard to compensation. Just suppose we get to the point where we know we want to work together. Is there a number in mind that you would love to have to join us, and [intentionally pause] also is there a realistic number you would accept?

The key to this question is calmness in your tone and patience in your cadence. You and Jane want to work together. This is not a negotiation but rather a collaboration to get to financial terms that both of you can work with to build a company together.

The question has an intentional structure and order. It asks her dream number first and then patiently asks for a realistic number.

Imagine that her dream number is something that fits within your budget. She will love that number and be elated. You now know that you can make that work if and when you decide to formalize an offer. Closing Jane to join you could not be easier in this scenario.

On the other hand, if her love/dream number is too far outside your budget, then this question opens a dialogue. You can be honest with Jane that her dream number won't work but approach her realistic number as something you want to work with so she can be excited to join your startup.

In either case, we have a "number that she would accept."

"I like that you see this conversation with Jane as a collaboration versus a negotiation. She and I can work out the financials so everyone is feeling valued. But what if her realistic number is way too high?"

Yeah, I hear you. Occasionally the star candidate will propose a number that outsizes your budget.

Typically, they have learned in MBA school the *anchoring technique*, in which they were taught to propose a number that they know is too high.

In other words, when they respond to the question they will propose an absurd dream number, but they will also state a realistic number that they know is too high.

They are trying to anchor you.

Their hope is you come down from this fake realistic number to their actual realistic number. A number that all along they knew they would accept. They just don't want to feel lowballed.

It's kind of a silly game.

What they should be taught is to be straightforward and not play games. In the end, it does not really work for either party.

You think they are playing a game, and they think you are trying to take advantage of them. The anchoring technique certainly won't work when collaborating on an offer with a responsible, intelligent founder like you.

Let's move on from my rant about the anchoring technique.

The great thing about having spent time on getting to know Jane as a person and not just an executive is, at this point, she should like you and trust you. She will know you care about her as a human being.

Within this vibe of safety and trust you can work with any number that Jane proposes. If her realistic number is too high, then work with Jane by explaining how her number is not doable. If she still won't budge, then don't continue this uphill climb. Accept that you won't be hiring Jane.

What is much more likely is this: by gently explaining your budget (or any other restriction), and proposing a number that works for both of you, Jane will accept the offer and join your startup.

Remember, the goal of trial closing is to make the formal presentation of an offer to Jane uneventful. You already know she will accept it because you worked through all of her concerns (including money) before the offer was presented.

On that note, let's chat about the final trial close topic.

Theme #5 – Making the Offer

The Magic of "Just Suppose"

The phrase "just suppose" is magical. You have already seen it applied in Theme #4. Now that you have a clear view of Jane's motivations related to money/risk, it is time to align expectations for receiving a formal offer to join your startup.

In a calm, easygoing tone, ask her the following:

Jane, being on the same page with you and working together to build a great company is really exciting, I cannot wait for you to get started. Just suppose the financial terms we discussed of _____ is approved by my partners and my board. Is there any reason you would not accept an offer to join us?

Listen. There may be an unexpected non-financial item that suddenly arises. This question flushes out any last-minute concerns. Examples could be medical benefits, life insurance, remote work possibility, pet care, prolonged start date, etc.

Expect something. It is normal for her to have one last concern, and it is the skilled founder who identifies that concern before presenting a formal offer.

At this stage, it is also important to verify details of Jane's compensation and credentials.

"Wait a minute. Isn't Jane going to feel that I don't trust her if I ask for her pay stub and proof that she graduated college?"

Yes and no. It depends on how you phrase and frame it. Say the following to her:

As you know, we run a thorough, structured recruitment process. It is something we really care about and, as you can tell, we are highly selective of who comes aboard our unique team. One of the last steps before you onboard with us is to verify your current compensation and college/MBA graduation. I will have our HR leader reach out separately to get this done with you. I just wanted to give you a heads up about that administrative part of our process.

Normally, the star executive will welcome this verification. They have nothing to hide; they have been honest about their compensation and educational history. You will only get pushback when there is a problem or a fear.

One example would be what they told you (or your team) is their current salary. Typically (and it is not necessarily a thing to worry about) executives round up their compensation. Happens all the time.

So, if someone told you they made a $100k salary, don't freak out when they actually make $99,200 a year. If they make $75K a year and they told you they make $100K, *then* you have a problem, and most likely this is not the kind of person you should hire. Because 75 never rounds up to 100.

Make sense? Terrific! Let's get back on track and wrap up the trial close.

Once you and Jane have worked through any lingering concerns she has by asking the "just suppose" question, ask her this next: *"Is there* anything else *that would prevent you from joining us?"*

Listen. There may be one last, random detail here to address.

"You are killing me. I cannot keep asking the same question! Jane is going to think I am a paranoid psychopath."

I know it's repetitive, but you have to ask. We don't want drama or surprises at the finish line. If you want to close like an elite recruiting founder, then ask . . . one . . . more . . . time.

As soon as you feel her concerns have been resolved, ask her the following question verbatim: *"Jane, do you want the job?"*

Direct questions get direct answers.

Ideally, she says, "Yes, I do."

From that point on, the negotiation of a formal offer will be easier, more fluid. Rarely does an executive say they want the job and not ultimately accept it.

In reality, she may respond in a variety of ways, including bringing up compensation again as an important factor before saying yes. Whatever objection she raises, it gives you another opportunity to overcome it.

This is the essence of trial closing—surfacing and resolving issues *prior* to a formal offer.

"Through these trial close questions—especially that key one asking Jane if she actually wants the job—I can uncover any remaining objections. Once I know her concerns, I have the opportunity to resolve them one by one directly with her. Once resolved, what do I do next? Do I make the verbal offer?"

Almost. At this point, Jane has told you she wants the job. Right before making the financial offer, I want you to ask Jane one last thing.

Start Date
Smile. Jane has told you she wants the job. The vibe should be positive, warm, and welcoming. Now, say to her:

Congratulations. How exciting you are joining us! Fantastic! What date can you start? Let's open our calendars now and pick your first day.

Be prepared for Jane to resist picking a specific date. Changing jobs is a nerve-wracking process even for star executives.

If she hesitates, take a step back, be steady, and calm your voice tone. Then, say this:

Take a day or two to think about the right start date for you. All of us are elated to have you on the team. I will call you end of the day tomorrow. Does 5:30 p.m. work? We can confirm your start date at that time.

I know I mentioned a day or two above. But you want to call her at the end of Day One to set the start date. Give space, but Jane does not need two days to think about it. Unfortunately, the phrase, "time kills all deals" is usually true.

Be smoothly insistent and organized. Don't let Jane overthink and complicate her resignation. Getting her commitment is about setting specific dates and confirming definite times to communicate. These steps are simply part of a good trial close process.

"I have to ask the trial close questions that gradually build up to asking Jane if she wants the job. I will be patient and firm to set a definite start date with her. But what do I do when she asks me about the actual financial offer? Won't she delay confirming a start date because she won't know the compensation she is agreeing to?"

Excellent question. First, you may be surprised how often a star candidate will agree to join you and set a start date even before you give them the financial details of your offer.

If they won't agree to a start date without knowing the compensation, then proceed to making the financial offer. Remember, we are simply trying to add another layer of commitment from Jane before we get to the numbers. If she wants numbers before setting a start date, no problem.

Here we go.

Show Me the Money

With offers, "one size fits all" does not exist. It really depends on the stage of your startup, the salary and package that Jane has, the market you operate in, your team's current comp, what is customary, etc.

Nevertheless, first-time founders should stick to what they can afford and act in the best interests of stakeholders. When making any financial offer, communicate with honesty and integrity. Be forthright about what you can and cannot pay.

Remember, Jane wants the job. Work with her to find a package that is equitable for all parties. Collaborate and start by saying a version of the following:

So excited I can count on you. Let's talk numbers. Here is what we can offer now.

Now, make your offer. Posture, poise, and present. Remain calm and patient when walking through the offer terms.

Expect her to question things here and there. In particular, you will need to be well-versed in explaining how your stock option plan and the option pool works.

Star candidates will typically request to see your capitalization table to know how they stack up compared to other C-level executives at your startup. This is normal behavior. Assume a rock star like Jane will ask for details.

In summary, be sensitive to Jane's current compensation,

your company's cash position, your capitalization table, and investors' needs, as well as any other relevant factors. You want to ensure that investing in Jane will not put your company's financial health in jeopardy.

Since you have followed my tips for creating connection with Jane, the presentation of the financial offer will be routine. The two of you already know you are going to work together. The offer is just a routine ritual to wrap up before she starts.

So long as you follow the trial close method, and have acted consistently in a trustworthy manner, she will sign the offer letter.

EXPERT TIP: When Jane responds that she wants the job, sets a start date with you, *and* is in agreement with financial terms, then rapidly send her a Docusign with terms of the offer (i.e., offer letter). Don't delay. You want fluidity in your closing process. Make obtaining her signature as easy as possible by making it electronic. No friction, easy to sign, and one click to send. In twenty years, only once have I seen an executive rescind an offer letter they signed. I am still surprised that it happened.

The Curious Candidate

During the interview process, you and the executive you are recruiting will have a lot of back and forth. When executing a good trial close you will be asking numerous direct questions. When done correctly, it is normal for the curious candidate to respond to one (or more) of your questions by asking, "Why are you asking me that?"

Your response should be authentic. Your intent, positive. Say the following:

What all of us care about is fit. I am asking you this question because I'd like you to feel an opportunity with us feels right and, of course, I owe that same feeling to my team, my board, my investors, and myself. I ask so you can trust you fit here. We are building something unique and it will only continue to be special if our culture remains one that is transparent, open, and honest with each other. Does that make sense?

Now, this response may not apply in all situations, but because it is heartfelt and sincere it should apply to most of them. As such, use these words as a guide, not as a rule.

The point is, we ask these trial questions to get to the truth. Who wouldn't want to be part of a culture where people can feel good about being truthful, direct, and themselves? It is refreshing.

KEY TAKEAWAY

By following my tips for trial closing, you can avoid unnecessary drama when recruiting game-changing executives. Running a startup is already challenging enough; don't make hiring rock star talent more difficult than it needs to be.

Chapter 9

DISCOVERY
THE POWER OF THE REFERENCE CHECK

Truth be told, reference checking is part of trial closing. Yet, it is such an important part of a best practice trial close that it deserves its own dedicated chapter.

Pay attention. Here's why reference checking gets special treatment.

Reference checking is more important
than interviewing.
—J. Patrick Gorman
(Yes, it's me. I have to have at least
one quote in my own book.)

Wait. If reference checking is the GOAT, then why did my team and I spend all this time interviewing?"

Great question. Interviewing *is* still important. Through it, you learn how an executive presents themselves and whether there's chemistry or not. You also get to absorb from your team a diverse set of opinions about the interviewee that sparks curiosity, fosters teamwork, and deepens judgment. All positive things.

However, if you don't complement your interviews with a proper reference check, then any hire is a risk. Combining a solid interview process plus a proper reference check is the gold standard for recruiting.

Let's dive into both why a reference check is so vital as well as detail how to do one (the right way).

Think about it. If I asked your mom to tell me about your personality versus a person you only went on two dates with, who is going to give me more insight?

You learn so much more about a star executive when you speak to someone who's worked with them for a significant amount of time.

The overarching purpose of reference checking is to understand what you are getting before the star executive starts. Every executive has weaknesses and blind spots. Understanding what they are, and if you and your team can manage and accept those flaws, is invaluable data to be conscious of prior to hiring this person.

Let's get dramatic so I can make my point.

Imagine if you were interviewing Bernie Madoff.

In person, he would have been irresistibly charming. Everyone would have wanted to hire Bernie.

However, would he have passed your reference check process? Think about it. If you had the opportunity to do a well-structured, deep-dive reference check on him with his co-workers you may have uncovered the scam artist that he actually was.

Make sense now? A proper reference check greatly diminishes the risk of making a bad hire.

Sigmund Freud said it best: "The self you know is hardly worth knowing." As he so poignantly demonstrates, our opinion of ourselves is of very little value. To best understand the executive being interviewed, first-time founders should learn what *other people* **say about this person.**

It is the opinion of others who have worked on a daily, weekly, and monthly basis with this executive that matters. Their collective work experience with him and subsequent viewpoint of him is, quite simply, his reputation.

Understanding the star executive's reputation is the fundamental reason you want to check his references before deciding to hire.

As demonstrated in the Madoff example, anyone can act the part in an interview. But through a structured reference check, you verify the executive's professional talent, values, and motivators.

Remember, we don't want actors. To avoid stagecraft, I'm going to detail three key steps. That way you can hire a star for work, not one for the stage.

STEP ONE: MINDSET

As mentioned, as a first-time founder it is critical to be in the right mental state prior to interviewing. This applies to reference checking too. Slow down, clear your mind, and be present before you begin. No distractions, no email, or WhatsApp interruptions. Be still, be present.

Presence also means that you are thinking about what's best for this executive *before* checking their references. It is only in this spirit of generosity that you can perform an effective reference check.

"It's beginning to sound like we are at a wellness retreat. Why all the hokey mindfulness here? I just want to learn how to do a solid reference check."

Because it is *so easy* for founders to try and make the executive fit rather than approaching the decision from the mindset of "what's best for this executive."

Recruiting is time consuming and exhausting for many founders. Most want to focus on technical product challenges and delighting customers; yet none of this is possible if you don't get the right people on your team. To do so, avoid getting caught up in the "rush to hire" mentality.

Think about it. When you meet someone who has "high potential," it can cloud your judgment. You rush the steps. You rush the process.

The risk in doing references in the wrong mindset is in looking for what you *want to hear versus what you want to learn about the executive. Learning about what makes the executive tick is essential data to guide your hiring decision. Being in the right frame of mind is a subtlety that makes a material difference when referencing an executive.*

Through mindfulness, you avoid the postmortem, bad hire "but that candidate had so much potential" speech.

STEP TWO: ENVIRONMENT

It is really hard to coordinate, but if you can pull it off, then do in-person reference checks.

In-person is the ideal environment because you are less likely to be distracted when you are sitting in front of a co-worker of the executive you are evaluating.

Moreover, when done in person, you realize how hard it is for this co-worker to disguise their body language when you start asking direct, coordinated questions.

Like most founders, you probably don't have time to find that chill coffee shop and sit for an hour (or more) with an executive's references. If this is the case, then do the next best thing and pick up the phone.

Performing reference checks telephonically is effective. But the key, in addition to mindset, is finding a quiet place where you will not be interrupted. It means you do not reply to texts, emails, or other calls during reference checks.

For 30–60 minutes you are not to be disturbed. Focus—you owe that to the interviewee, yourself, your team, your board, your investors, and your customers.

EXPERT TIP: It sounds obvious but the next time you do a reference check be conscientious of your surroundings. Case in point, the next time someone calls you to do a reference about someone who worked for you, be aware of how distracted the caller is. They most likely are just going through the motions and are not present on the call. Don't make this error when reference checking for your startup.

Enter and safeguard an environment of peace. A place where you will be able to deeply listen for the subtleties in pitch and tone of the person giving the reference. Be still, be patient, be present.

Most importantly, listen for nuance.

Nuance is everything. Often, how something is said, or what is *not* said, provides the clearest picture of the executive you are assessing.

EXPERT TIP: Avoid doing a reference check through email or WhatsApp. It is too hard to gain context from written communication in comparison to oral.

STEP THREE: STRUCTURE IS SUCCESS

Now that you are calm and in a tranquil environment it is time to ask the key questions that form a structured, succinct, and effective reference check.

For illustrative purposes, let's assume again the executive you are reference checking is Jane Smith. Follow these ten lines of questioning:

Question 1
- How do you know Jane? What is her business relationship to you? How long have you known her?

A solid reference check starts with understanding the context. As a first-time founder, do not assume that the former boss of Jane Smith hired her or has supervised her for years and years. The questions above ensure the content you hear has relevance by establishing the breadth and depth of Jane's relationship to the reference.

Imagine her former boss telling you he only supervised her work for a couple of weeks. The quality of insight gained will not be the same as a long-term supervisor.

Question 2
- Tell me about Jane's work. What one project did she do that tells me all I need to know about her work product.

Listen for teamwork, a bias for action and results, resourcefulness, fast learner. Understand how long the project took and what was the result. What was Jane's specific role and what skills did the reference see "in action." Are these skills what your startup needs now? If not, don't hire Jane.

Question 3

- Now, tell me about working with Jane. In your opinion, what would these *different groups of people say about her interpersonal ability?*
  - **Supervisors** *(Does Jane challenge authority in a good way? Is she sycophantic? Is she afraid to deliver bad news?)*
  - **Peers** *(Is Jane collaborative or is she a climber who will use others to get ahead?)*
  - **Staff** *(Pay particular attention to comments here. If your startup starts scaling rapidly, how Jane manages teams will be a critical factor in your ability to grow.)*
  - **Customer/Supplier/Client** *(Is it a partnership? Is she too much of a people-pleaser? Can she negotiate well? Does she bring results?)*

Question 4

- Of all the things Jane does well, what 1–2 adjectives describe her strengths?

Is there alignment with her strengths and what your startup needs over the next 1–5 months? It's critical to always keep the short-term needs of your startup in mind. A startup company lives and dies on its ability to respond quickly to change. Make sure the star executive's skill set fills the need that your startup has *now*, not 1–2 years from now.

Are these the same strengths that you noted during your interviews with Jane?

Question 5

- All of us have things we can improve upon. What about Jane? What 1–2 things could she do better?

Remember, anytime you ask a question that seeks to know "negative" things about another person it should be framed in a way that gives the reference permission to be open with you. Lessen their defensiveness.

By saying that all of us have weaknesses, you are showing that we are all imperfect. You are not looking to harm Jane's career but rather make a judgment as to whether or not her weaknesses are things that you can manage at work (and still thrive).

As you listen to the reference describe Jane's weaknesses, be sure to understand if these "defects" have persisted or if Jane has improved on them over time. You want to hire executives who learn quickly, are adaptive, and have that growth mindset for your new startup. Not those stuck in the same problematic behavior.

Question 6

• Are there any ethical issues with Jane? Would you and your team tell me she is an honest person?

This might be the most important question you ask. *Values are everything.* It is hard enough to build a company from scratch. Imagine doing it with teammates who have questionable ethics.

If there is any answer here that hints at Jane being dishonest, then slow down and probe to understand the context. If there is a tangible example of questionable behavior, then include this example when asking about Jane's ethics with others from her reference list.

Be sure to use the words "you and your team" to uncover if there is someone else this reference knows who would think Jane is dishonest. If that comes up, probe to gain context.

Question 7
- Of all the people you have worked with in your career, tell me about Jane as a performer.

Listen, then ask:

- Where does she rank on a scale of 1 to 10? 1 being the worst person you ever worked with and 10 being the very best.

This question seems clichéd, but the responses will undoubtedly be insightful. *If Jane is a 6 or less, you have a problem.* What is Jane missing? Usually, a 6 or lower is not someone you hire. However, it is important to compare this rating of 6 with Jane's other references. If everyone ranks her a 6 or lower, then don't hire Jane.

If Jane is a 7, then ask, "Why not an 8?" And if Jane is a 10, then ask, "Why not an 11?" Always ask the reference why they did not rank Jane one point higher to uncover what Jane needs to improve on. Is what she needs to improve on consistent with the responses this reference provided for Question 5?

Question 8
Similar to Question 7, we have a two-part sequence.

Part One
- Would you hire Jane again?

Even if the reference is not senior enough to hire Jane, ask the question. If the reference states that they are not in a position to hire Jane, then ask, "If you *were* able to make that decision, would you hire her?"

Cut to the chase. If the reference hesitates to hire Jane again, then understand what Jane lacks to be welcomed back. If they would not hire her again, why would you?

<u>Part Two</u>
- Imagine today you decided to quit your job and start your own company for the very first time. Considering all the risk, excitement, and craziness of a new startup, would you hire Jane to join your company from Day 1?

It is one thing to hire Jane back to her former employer. It is completely different for the reference to think through the frame of Jane in a startup (more importantly, *their* startup). If they would not hire Jane for their own startup, why would you hire Jane for yours?

If they would hire Jane, then ask, "For what role?" You may be shocked that it would be a different role than the role you are evaluating Jane for.

Question 9
- As you can imagine, hiring Jane is a critical decision for my partners and me. Is there anything I missed? In other words, what else about Jane should I have asked you?

If there is additional information make sure to follow it up by saying, "Tell me more." These three words unlock what this reference really wants you to know about Jane.

Question 10
- Have you ever thought about joining a startup?

As a first-time founder, become a world-class recruiter. Elite recruiters ask the questions that others are afraid to. From time to time, one of Jane's references will possess the skill set that your startup needs. Why not ask if they would be open to learning more about you and your company's plans?

Hiring the best talent is not easy. Don't make it harder by excluding a highly qualified executive just because they are a reference for the executive you are evaluating. Ironically, this reference person may end up being a better fit than the executive you interviewed!

Be diplomatic. Be sensitive. You don't want Jane to think you are being overly aggressive. At the same time, don't apologize for hiring the best people for your startup.

Timing Is Everything

"I now see how important it is to complement a strong interview process with a well-structured reference check to avoid a Bernie Madoff–type hire. But when do I ask the executive to provide me with a list of references? In the first interview? After I have made a verbal offer?"

Terrific question. There is no hard-and-fast rule of when you should ask an executive for their professional references. But typically you (or a member of your team) will ask for this list at the end of your interview process and right before you are prepared to make an offer.

When asking for their reference list be prepared for some pushback, especially if the candidate has not told anyone that they are interviewing at your startup. Typically, an executive will express concern about confidentiality since she or he has not received (nor accepted) an offer to join you.

When this happens, you'll be happy you followed my advice in previous chapters to build trust. Because, at this point, the star executive sitting before you is confident you would never intentionally do anything to harm their career.

The next step is to assure this executive that you will keep these reference calls confidential. Then, you will also ask this star executive to request that the people on his reference list keep his candidacy confidential. Everyone is hanging out in the "trust tree." Normally, people are professional, discreet, and will not break the confidentiality of this star executive.

EXPERT TIP: Typically, executives will provide a list of references that they believe will only say positive things about them. If you utilize my recommended questions and mindset tips above, you may be surprised at how much "negative" information these "friends" of the executive will provide to you. Remember, your goal is to find out what is best for the executive you are considering for hire. Hopefully, your reference checking concludes that this star executive is a good fit. However, a well-done reference check may also uncover things about this executive that are too difficult to manage and, therefore, make him the wrong candidate for your startup.

EXPERT TIP: Be careful and decide cautiously. But when speaking to those on the reference list, ask them about other people who have worked with the executive you are assessing. These "off list" co-workers, suppliers, bosses, staff people, etc. will amplify your ability to assess fit.

Just be careful not to break the executive's confidentiality. Mention to this star executive that part of your reference-checking process will inevitably lead to speaking to people who are not on their original list of references. When sharing this, expect pushback from the star executive again. Your voice tone is calm, and your message is consistent. Express that you understand how important discretion is and that you will ask all references to keep the conversations confidential.

"I get it. But when I tell them I will speak to people not on their list, won't that seem creepy and weird? Won't the executive I am evaluating worry that their current employer will find out they are interviewing with me?"

Yes, you are correct. There is always a risk that confidentiality will get broken if someone squeals to the executive's current employer that they are interviewing with you.

However, it could very well happen that someone on their original list does the same type of squealing. Assure the executive how important their confidentiality is, and that you will stress to anyone you speak to how important their anticipated discretion is as well. Most people won't breach an executive's confidentiality, especially if they are asked not to. In most cases, it would be embarrassing for everyone involved if they agreed to confidentiality and then broke their pledge.

EXPERT TIP: Say the following to the on *and* off-list references: "Imagine if it got out to your boss that you were talking to me about an opportunity with us. How would you feel? It would be very embarrassing, so please keep our chat confidential. Does that make sense?" When explaining it this way (putting this person in the shoes of the executive being evaluated), rest assured that most people will remain discreet.

EXPERT TIP: It is crucial to record every reference on a 1–2 page PDF document. These documents should be added to the executive's file and shared with the relevant parties within your startup. Archiving this data may be helpful later when deciding on a new role/position for this executive. I chose PDF so that the original document cannot be easily altered by others.

KEY TAKEAWAY

Mindset, calm space, and adequate, undistracted time to listen are the foundational elements for a successful reference check. Layered on top of this sturdy base are the ten core lines of questioning to ensure a good hire.

I get it, routine is boring. Most people resist following a process. It is much easier to "hope for the best." But it is this very process that will bring insight into the real personality, the actual skill set, and the genuine teamwork ability of the executive you are evaluating. If you can commit to following these steps, I guarantee the quality of your team will grow and the ease with which you hire future star executives will be admired by your team and reviled by your competitors.

PART THREE

RECRUITING ROADBLOCKS (AND SOLUTIONS)

Chapter 10
I, OBJECT
COMMON OBJECTIONS
TO ACCEPTING YOUR OFFER

At this point in the recruitment process, let's assume the following:

- You've run a well-structured, thoughtful interview process.
- You've asked the trial close questions and feel comfortable that "Jane Smith" (our CFO star executive) wants the job and is someone you want to hire.
- Jane's references were fantastic and you want to hire her.

Excited, you think you have her acceptance in the bag . . . until Jane voices one of the...

Top Five Objections to Accepting Your Offer

Before you can pop the celebratory champagne, let's examine each potential objection, along with how to best counter, to ensure Jane wisely elects to come work for your startup.

Objection #1—"I am not in a rush."

Get ready founders, you are going to hear this one all the time.

In the startup world, every day counts. Time is your most valuable asset but, oftentimes, the executive sitting across from you has been conditioned to respond with this objection because of something you are doing, saying, or conveying. This vibe is making them feel too uncomfortable to join your startup. As such, remember how important it is to use your voice as a soothing instrument when recruiting stars. Think calm, late-night DJ voice. Your tone and posture should resonate that everything is under control.

When you hear the star executive voice this common objection, respond gently by asking, "Do you think you will stay at your current company forever?"

If she responds, *"Yes, I will probably stay for my entire career,"* then move on. This executive is perusing and will not join your startup.

"*Whoa.* . . Here we go again. You are too quick to dismiss these people as viable candidates for my startup. Is it really that dramatic? I just write this star executive off?"

I think it best to respond with a quote:
I am not always right, but I am never wrong.
—Corey Wayne

Admittedly, there are exceptions to the rule. However, if a top executive tells you they plan to stay their whole career at their current employer, then believe them. For whatever reason, they are not enthused about what you are building. Dedicate your time to those who, at the very least, give you the notion they want "in."

Sometimes, the star candidate will respond another way and say, *"No, I won't stay there forever"* or *"Forever is a long time."* When you hear this from a star candidate, reply as follows: "What is missing where you work that makes you open to leaving?"

Your response is subtle but intentional.

You actually want to say, verbatim, "open to leaving." Because you are planting the seed for his departure.

Furthermore, by asking "what is missing" you will now hear details about what would motivate him to join your startup.

Once you know what is missing, be brutally honest with yourself. Does your startup fill that gap? If not, then don't try and make it work. Great founders don't embrace false hope, nor do they sell it. With kindness, encourage this executive to find a better fit elsewhere.

But if your company *does* fill that gap, then by all means highlight this differentiator. Make it clear how your startup differs from his current employer. This differentiator becomes the catalyst to spark this star executive to "be in a rush," resign from his current job, and join your startup.

When you ask about "forever," you alter the executive's context of time and inspire his bias for action. The question makes him feel that he could be wasting time by working somewhere he knows is not forever.

When this happens, who wouldn't be "in a rush" to find a better fit?

Hopefully, the best fit is at your startup.

Objection #2—"I have not yet completed my cycle."

The origin of this excuse must have begun at one of the big consulting or investment banks as a cunning way to prevent losing their star executives.

When employers counsel their star staff to complete their cycle, it could mean waiting for a promotion, finishing a project, or both. What they are really saying is, *"You can leave, just not now."*

What this truly means is you can leave on their terms and their timeline, not yours.

To be clear, I am not advocating for people to leave their employers high and dry.

What I am advocating for is to *keep it real.* Goldman Sachs, Microsoft, McKinsey, etc. are not going to close down because one of their star executives joins your startup.

The risk is that the star executive feels guilty, stays too long at their current employer, and misses out on that incredible opportunity to build a company from 0 to 1 with you—all because they were trying to complete some magical, mystical "cycle."

To illustrate, let's throw it back to July 5, 1994. Bellevue, Washington. Jeff Bezos's garage.

Imagine Jeff has just finished extending an offer to that star Goldman Sachs banker to be his first CFO. Expecting a yes, he instead hears, *"Jeff, I would love to join you, but I think I still need to complete my cycle at Goldman."*

Undoubtedly, this executive who chose to "finish the cycle" is probably still kicking himself for passing on Amazon in 1994.

As the next Jeff Bezos, the best way for you to counter this excuse is by exposing reality: cycles, projects, and new deals never end at most companies. (Unless, of course, the company itself shuts down. In this scenario, the executive you want to recruit will not voice the objection about completing their cycle.)

Before this executive completes project A, he will be assigned to project B, midstream. His cycle can literally go on and on and on; it never ends. The moment will never be right to leave.

So the next time you hear the executive you are recruiting

voice the "cycle" excuse, ask them, "Would the company you work for go out of business if you left tomorrow?"

If they say yes, then let them complete the cycle! They are working on one of those critical, time-sensitive projects that need their time and attention. (In this scenario, you should then ask for their timeline. When will this critical project come to a conclusion? Make a note in your calendar to follow up with them again two weeks *before* the project's expected conclusion. Try again to recruit them at that time.)

If they say no, then ask, "That is really good to know—nobody wants where you work to shut down. Now suppose you keep meeting our team, our investors, and you know in your heart you want to join us. Would you be open to finding a way for us to make this work?"

Pause and listen.

If he says *no*, then move on. Also, if there is any hesitation, move on, too. Applying your "never give up" attitude does not always work when recruiting elite talent. Sometimes you have to move on even though you will be tempted to double-down on your recruitment efforts.

Besides, you want someone enthused about your vision, who just needs a little help navigating their departure from their current employer.

If he says *yes,* then say, "How exciting! We are going to build an unforgettable company together. What 2–3 ideas do you have that will help you to resign gracefully and join us?"

You intentionally want to:

- reinforce building something sensational
- ask for collaboration to guide their departure
- remark that they are resigning

Don't be jerky. Be calm. Remember my advice on having that soothing DJ voice.

Don't force things now. Let this star executive leave their employer the right way before onboarding with you. It may require an extended start date but, in the long run, hiring a game-changer is worth the wait.

Objection #3—"I want to manage a P&L."

You know who you are. You went to Harvard MBA or Stanford GSB or one of the other top ten MBA programs. You are insanely bright. You work in consulting or banking at Meta, Adobe, or Apple. You dress well, and you speak well.

We met, you talked, I listened. You told me you wanted to join a startup, make a difference, leave a legacy, take some risk, make it big etc., and then you said one . . . more . . . thing...

"Also, I want to manage a P&L."

First reaction—ugh.

Second reaction—double ugh.

Here me out. I am not against anyone becoming a CEO and/or running a business unit with responsibility for the P&L. It is my profession to recruit C-level executives.

What concerns me is startup fit.

As a first-time founder, be wary when you hear the person sitting across from you utter this phrase. Typically, it signals risk aversion. This type of person tends to focus on climbing, step by step, the predictable corporate ladder rather than building a company with you from the ground up.

To counter the P&L objection say the following:

"Running a P&L is certainly a big responsibility. Yet, building a company from scratch offers a similar but more unique experience. You want to lead, I get that. Is there a better school for leadership than going from 0 to 1? Ask Bill Gates. Ask Mark Zuckerberg. Ask anyone who has done it. There's nothing like it."

Pause and listen. If the executive seems bored, then move on. They are not the right personality for your startup.

Conversely, if the executive seems curious then say the following:

"If you want to run a P&L, then first learn to build a business. Look, your expertise today may be in marketing, but six months from now you will be able to share experiences from operations, sales, product, and programming, as well as fundraising, facilities, and recruiting. Everyone in the beginning pitches in. It is that diverse experience that is invaluable if one day you want to run the show."

By its nature, your startup will challenge its leadership team to be agile, adept, perform under pressure, and navigate constraints while at the same time recruiting talent, budgeting and forecasting, raising money, and experimenting to find product/market fit. It should be obvious to the curious executive that these skills are directly correlated to their goal of running a P&L.

Objection #4—"I just got promoted, so I have to stay."

Much like the response to "I am not in a rush," you want to counter this excuse by getting them to see their career through a long-term lens.

Reply upbeat with, "What wonderful news. Will you now stay there forever?"

If the star executive replies yes, then pause your recruitment process for now. Wish them well and mark your calendar to call them in 2–3 months.

Why call this executive later on? *Because company cultures don't change.* It is a safe bet that this executive's motives to change from their current company to your startup will remain even after their promotion.

As a founder, embody the attitude of a winner's mindset that this promotion is simply a temporary setback to your ability to recruit this star executive in the near future. You may be surprised at how excited they are to join you when you reach out 2–3 months later; they were just waiting for your call.

On the other hand, if they say no, signaling that they won't stay forever, then say, "Makes sense; you are being consistent and thoughtful. Your promotion confirms what we always knew: you are a great talent. Let's get to work building a remarkable business together. When will you tell them you have joined us?"

This question uncovers the guilt factor.

If the star executive agrees to resign, then set in motion their onboarding process.

However, it typically won't be that easy. It is almost guaranteed the star executive is going to feel guilty about resigning after just getting promoted (or receiving other forms of recognition like a big raise, a retention bonus, or a new stock grant).

If, at this point, you can feel that guilt/worry from them, then say, "I could be wrong. By joining us, aren't you being loyal to what is best for you?"

Pause and listen. If they don't agree, then move on. Focus your energy on a more decisive executive. If they do agree, then continue with the following: "That is what I thought. Sometimes it is hard to trust yourself, right?"

Pause and listen. If it still feels like they want to join you, then say calmly, "Today you are going to need to have that hard conversation with the people who promoted you. It won't be easy, but you will grow from it. Right before you say goodbye, remind yourself of your sound judgment. They would not have promoted you without it, and you would not have accepted my offer without using it. Good luck and text me afterward so I know you survived [*laugh to break the tension, keeping your overall tone light*]. I cannot wait to work together."

There is always a risk that this star executive will decide to stay at their current employer, but oftentimes they just need to feel your belief in them to find the words to say goodbye.

Objection #5—"*I always wanted to start my own company. One day for sure I will, but my kids are in private school, and I cannot afford to take the risk right now.*"

There are various versions of this excuse. The star executive will share that they want to take the risk of building a startup, but *the timing* is not right. They will blame their kids, their mortgage, their MBA debt, etc. for their inability to make the move now.

It is the classic "but one day" excuse.

Be patient and calm when you hear it. Breathe. Be empathetic. Not everyone understands wealth and, as the founder and leader of your startup, you must now play the role of teacher. Reply with, "I get it. You have a lot *of responsibility financially*; it is not easy to balance it all. I don't know how you do it, but it looks like you always find a way. If it's okay with you, let's keep it simple: Do you want to join us?"

Pause and listen.

If this executive returns to complaining about money, then it is best to move on. She is too risk averse to join a startup and, take my word for it, she will never start her own business. There will never be a "right" time. She is too prudent.

If, on the other hand, she reverts to showing genuine enthusiasm for your startup, then don't lose her over money fears.

You have a couple of different options that apply as the situation dictates:

Offer Terms

Is there a way for you to tweak her offer so that she gets more salary and less equity? Can you guarantee her a raise after your next funding round? Work through possible scenarios with her to make it work. Again, this assumes you have financial flexibility.

No Financial Flexibility but High Potential for Wealth

If you are at a point in your startup where you cannot be flexible with cash, then shift focus to the upside of your stock's potential. Become the "Professor of Wealth" and ask her, "Who is the richest person you know?"

Pause and listen.

Almost every time that I have asked this question the executive replies that the richest person they know is an owner. Rich people own assets that produce riches. Being an owner is the path to great wealth.

Go ahead and try and find an ultrawealthy person who got that way through their salary. You won't.

As she shares with you details of the richest person she knows, focus on how they became that way. Typically, it will follow that same familiar pattern—they are an owner. Wealthy people own assets. Assets produce wealth.

From this example, walk her through "realistic" as well as "best-case" scenarios with what her equity (an asset) could be worth to her in the future. Remind her how proud her family and friends will be of her courage to invest in herself, build something, and most importantly follow her own unique path.

Don't we all admire people like that?

KEY TAKEAWAY

Most people live and work in fear. Unfortunately, we are conditioned to worry more about what we can lose than what we can win. By being in a constant state of fear, most star executives resist the upside of startups.

The objections and counter-responses laid out above should be understood in this context. Because embracing this context *identifies false hope*.

Whenever it feels too difficult to recruit an executive, embrace reality and stop recruiting them. It is better to focus your time and energy on those who are enthused by your mission and vision.

In that rare instance when you see a twinkling of possibility that the executive sitting across from you is open to taking the leap to your startup, go for it by nudging them.

Yes. Nudge them.

To nudge is to employ reason, persuasion, logic, and curiosity, so that the executive you want to hire sees the light. Instead of becoming a victim of her excuses, she listens, adapts, and embraces her ambition.

Just like you did.

Chapter 11
THE INEVITABLE COUNTEROFFER

Congratulations! After following my process for an effective trial, you and rock-star executive Jane worked through her concerns and wrapped up all the details of her offer. She looked you in the eye, shook your hand, and gave you her word that she is joining.

You set a specific start date, told your team and investors that Jane is coming aboard, and even updated your PowerPoint marketing documents by adding her bio in your org chart. Fundraising just got a whole lot easier now that you have Jane starting in a couple weeks.

Your phone vibrates. You check your texts, and there it is. A brief message from Jane: *Can we talk? I think I have changed my mind.*

Your heart drops, your palms sweat, and a shiver moves down your spine. You think, *Is this really happening? Jane gave me her word! I told the board!*

If it makes you feel any better I almost named this chapter: *"Be Worried If the Star Executive You are Recruiting Does Not Receive a Counteroffer."*

The elite recruiter never assumes anything.

The elite recruiter is always learning and listening.

The elite recruiter also knows that the brighter the star a candidate is, the higher the likelihood they'll receive a tempting counteroffer. It's par for the course, part of the game.

"Okay, I will expect any high-quality professional that I am recruiting to receive counteroffer pressure to stay at their current employer. But how do I counterattack? How can I make sure 'Jane' starts as our new CFO?"

Addressing counteroffers should happen *twice* during your interview process. First, when the candidate is walking you through her job history, and second after she has verbally accepted your offer.

Job History

Ask Jane, "During any of these job moves did you ever receive a counteroffer? Did you accept it? Would you do that again?"

Bringing up counteroffers in the beginning phases of the interview process is *mandatory*. It is best practice for a good trial close.

If Jane has previously taken a counteroffer and thinks it was a mistake, she will be much less likely to repeat that behavior with your offer.

If she *is* still open to counteroffers, then be thankful you asked about the topic early on in your interview process. You now have time to address it with her face to face. You are now also prepared to address it again if and when you actually make her a verbal offer.

After She Has Verbally Accepted Your Offer

When Jane goes to tell her boss that she is leaving, expect mayhem. The angst her boss feels in losing Jane may be greater than the emotion of joy you feel in hiring her! As a result, expect her boss to act with desperation, offering her more money, more stock, more vacation, a promotion, a transfer, a company car, etc., in the hopes that she'll stay.

When this happens stay calm and say the following to Jane:

"I know how hard it is to leave a place where you have done great work. When we started this interview process you and I both knew they would very likely attempt a counteroffer. I am not at all surprised and I'd bet neither are you. We knew this would happen."

Listen and wait. Give Jane a chance to say that she is not going to take the counteroffer.

If Jane responds that she is confused and is considering the counteroffer, then say the following in a tone of positivity and tranquility:

"Well, I certainly understand how much pressure you must feel to stay. You have earned a terrific reputation and that is one of the many reasons we are excited for your start with us. Look, last week you gave me your word that you wanted to join us. For me, you never would have committed to us if that is not what you really wanted. Trust yourself."

Listen and wait. Jane may recommit to you right then and there.

If she stays committed to joining your startup, make sure to take her for breakfast or lunch prior to her actual start date. Set it up as a welcome meeting where you will chat briefly about work items but mostly want to spend time congratulating her and making sure you are available to make her transition easier. Don't bring up the counteroffer at this meal. Focus on the present not the past.

If she is still showing doubts, then end the conversation by saying the following:

"I know it takes a lot of courage to follow through on your commitment to us. Sleep on it, follow your heart, and call me tomorrow at 8 a.m. Thank you, Jane, I am really happy we can communicate so well. It is going to be incredible to build something together. I will speak to you tomorrow at 8."

Remember, rarely does an executive say yes and not follow through. You want to be understanding and "in control" of the outcome. By making her "sleep on it," you show control, posture, and patience. You come across to Jane as confident in yourself and in her original decision to join you. You are not needy.

Remember, Jane wants the job; she just needs a gentle nudge to say goodbye to her current employer.

If for some reason she decides to take the counteroffer, be polite and accepting. As much as you wanted Jane on your team, realize that there are other star executives out there who can also bring massive impact to your startup.

Ironically, most executives who take counteroffers will be back on the market within a few months. If you are still interested in hiring Jane, then reach out to her 2–3 months after she accepts the counteroffer. You may be surprised at how excited she is that the door of opportunity to contribute her game-changing talent to your startup is still open.

EXPERT TIP: When the timing is right, my recommendation would be to share Paul Hawkinson's counteroffer articles. Copy and paste them into a PDF and ask the executive to read through the articles. Hawkinson's articles explain why accepting a counteroffer is almost always a terrible idea. Here is a link to two of his articles on the topic:

https://www.purcellintl.com/WSJ-CounterOffer.pdf

https://npaworldwide.com/blog/resources/
counteroffer-acceptance-road-to-career-ruin/

Chapter 12
WHY WOULD ANYONE HIRE A HEADHUNTER?

"Now that I have read *Recruit the Remarkable*, why would I ever need to hire a headhunter? I just need to follow your lessons, correct?"

Well, here's the thing. You can study finance at Wharton, but being on a Wall Street trading desk is another level.

They call it the real world for a reason.

It's the same thing for elite recruiting. When you meet a headhunter who is reputable and has a stellar track record, hire him for the master class. You have studied my tips, but by hiring a star recruiter you get a front row seat to observe the concepts in action.

Is it necessary? No. But, do it to shorten your learning curve.

"Makes sense. I can accelerate my path to becoming an elite recruiter by hiring and observing a top headhunter do an executive search for me. But when is the best time to hire this headhunter? How do I choose the right one? And how does it all work (e.g., fees, timeline, warranties, etc.)?"

Timing

Most founders will call a headhunter months after they have started recruiting for a role. They will have tapped out their network and need the headhunter to amplify their reach.

Let's first review the typical sources a founder will reach out to in order to hire talent. Unfortunately, these sources *usually don't work* to recruit A-list executives.

MBA Friends

A founder's MBA classmates are smart, talented people but most of these folks are risk averse. Think about it. Why did they go to MBA school instead of starting their own company? You don't need an MBA to launch a business.

The pool of risk-taking MBAs certainly exists (Cristina Junqueira, Edward Wible, and David Vélez of Nubank are terrific examples). However, a founder with a Harvard MBA may only have relationships in that small pool of Harvard risk-seeking graduates. Furthermore, these rare, risk-seeking Harvard MBAs may be more focused on launching their own startups than joining yours.

Through a top headhunter you can gain access to a broader group of risk-seeking MBAs. Because a skilled headhunter will have relationships with all the top MBA programs, not just the school you graduated from. Also, this headhunter knows which MBAs are risk seeking and which are not.

Venture Capital Investors

A great VC knows everyone. Also, a great VC has sound judgment. These two attributes combine to help top VCs cultivate relationships with deeply talented executives who can positively impact your startup.

However, how does that VC decide who she will introduce

a star CTO to when she has 30–40 different founders in her portfolio who would love to meet the same star CTO?

The scenario is workable but prone to conflict.

If she outsources the relationship with this CTO to her in-house HR person, is the relationship between VC investor and star executive diluted? Won't this star CTO want the attention directly from the VC investor and not her HR team?

As you have learned, people want to feel special. Egos can be hard to navigate without that direct personal touch.

A top headhunter rarely has such conflicts to manage. Moreover, when retained to exclusively represent your startup, the headhunter can focus his time to serve you and not the 30–40 competing startups who want a rock-star CTO's attention for potential employment.

At the very least, a proven headhunter is dealing directly with the star CTO, is spending 100 percent of their workday focused on recruiting; they can dedicate the necessary time to make sure any recruiting conflicts are eloquently managed, understood, and accepted by all parties.

The bottom line is that talent matching and executive recruiting are only part of a VC's responsibility. As such, be aware of this limitation and manage your expectations when a VC claims that they are experts at executive recruiting. They may know who the best executives are, but it does not mean they can consistently source them to your startup.

LinkedIn

It is completely possible to recruit a star executive from this well-known platform. Problem is, most founders don't have time nor have they been taught how to effectively use LinkedIn to inbound the best executives.

Additionally, LinkedIn is full of executives who have exaggerated their qualifications—which again presents the problem of time for founders. Filtering and screening hundreds of LinkedIn executives can be mind-numbing and time-consuming for founders.

Hiring a top headhunter shifts that time commitment and responsibility to their domain of expertise. They know how to filter. They know how to say no to the wrong candidates. And they know how to persuade the resistant ones who could be just right for your startup.

You, as the founder, can concentrate on interviewing their curated list of talented executives instead of trying to qualify candidates all on your own.

Other Founders

A quality source of executives can come from the generosity of other founders. For example, some founders you know may have met a top CFO, but because they did not need to hire her at the time, she becomes available to you.

However, relying on other founders is not a good strategy simply because other founders will prioritize solving the myriad of challenges at their own startups. They don't have the bandwidth to help you. It won't be their priority.

Then you have the founders who are shortsighted and won't help you. They prefer to keep their "short list" of superstar executives to themselves. They want the first option to hire these people when the need arises at their own startup. Like little children, they don't want to share.

I don't think this happens often, but you will see some founders bickering over "poaching" and other catty conversations where they think they "own" a person's employment decisions. Counting on this type of founder to source for you is a waste of time.

Interestingly, by hiring a top headhunter you can maintain cordial relationships with fellow founders. Think about the following scenario:

A founder you met at a conference introduces you to a star CFO who he adores. You meet the person, but they are not the right culture fit for your startup. How do you tell the founder who made the introduction that this CFO is not a not a cultural fit for your startup? You can imagine how that could sting her ego if she receives your feedback as a snub.

However, when you have retained a headhunter, you can tell that founder your headhunter declined the executive she introduced, not you. What an easy way to save face.

By delegating the search process to the headhunter, you eliminate those time-sucking conversations about why you said no to candidates referred to you directly.

All in all, the decision to hire a top headhunter is up to you, but if you decide to do it, then my suggestion is do it on Day 1 of the search. Why delay meeting star executives?

Let's keep going with the other headhunter-related topics you are likely curious about.

Fees

Most elite headhunters charge a retainer. Like a lawyer, you are retaining that headhunter's time to focus on your search.

There is no "rule" as to what the fees will be, but it typically ranges from 25–33 percent of the executive's annual cash compensation (salary + target cash bonus). For example, let's say the executive you hire is paid $100K annual salary and a $20K target cash bonus. If the headhunter's fee is 33 percent your total fee would be one-third of $120K, or $40K.

Usually, a retainer is paid upfront to start the search. This retainer is deducted from the final fee of $40K. So, in the example above, a typical retainer amount would be $15K. Therefore, the remaining fee to be paid would be $25K.

This $25K is typically paid in two installments. The first installment ($12.5K) is paid when you start interviewing the headhunter's "short-listed" executives, and the remaining $12.5K is paid when the executive starts working for you.

There are many variations to how retainers and fees are calculated, but the framework explained here is common. Expect some variation of the following: a portion of the overall fee charged upfront to retain the headhunter to start your search (the retainer) and then 2–3 installments of the remaining fee paid as specific milestones in the search process are achieved.

Warranty Period

Every top headhunter will have a warranty period. This means that for a period of time (typically 6–12 months) the executive they placed at your startup is guaranteed to stay at your company.

If you fire the executive or the executive quits before the warranty period has expired, then the headhunter will not charge another retainer but instead agree to "redo" the same search.

A guarantee like this hardly ever needs to be enforced. Great headhunters rarely miss. They know what they are doing and, just like a top lawyer, they know how to win the case.

Minimum Fee Clause

Most startups don't have the budget to match the high salaries and cash bonuses of the executives they are trying to recruit for their startups. To compete, founders market the potential upside of their stock options.

As a result, expect headhunters who specialize in helping startups to include a minimum cash fee in their contract: this is because it can get complicated trying to value what stock options will be worth and subsequently charge a percentage of that value. If your startup becomes a unicorn, and the executive's stock is worth 10 million USD, are you going to pay the headhunter 3.3 million dollars? I don't think so.

Bottom line, expect the headhunter to include a minimum fee clause in their contract. It is their attempt to find an equitable way to be compensated fairly for their time to recruit a star executive on your behalf.

"I see that I should expect to pay a substantial cash fee to hire a top headhunter. But how can I make sure that I am getting my money's worth? I don't want to end up empty-handed and feel that my money was wasted."

I totally get it. Makes a lot of sense. Let me present…

How to Ensure You Hire the Right Recruiter Who Delivers

Having read this book, you now have an advantage. You have learned tips, methods, and processes to recruit at your best. You can recruit this star executive without the outside help of a top recruiter.

But sometimes you won't have the time. So, let's get tactical in your search for the *right* recruiter (to make your life easier).

Be Prepared for Him to Say "No"

Usually, the best recruiters won't have the capacity to help you. They are always busy and in high demand. Other times, they won't feel you are a good bet for their reputation, and they will say no. Don't take it personally, and don't try and offer the star headhunter an even bigger fee.

Offering a larger fee reinforces his impression you are needy, desperate, and not a good fit. It will turn him off—a great head-hunter is not for sale.

Instead, ask what is missing for him to feel comfortable rep-resenting you. Seek feedback even if it is painful. It opens the door for you to work together in the future.

If he cannot help you now, then ask who he would recom-mend to help you recruit a star executive. A talented headhunter is obsessed with his reputation so you can trust that whomever he recommends will be a recruiter of high quality.

Track Record Is More Important Than Chemistry

Don't be fooled that you must "like" the headhunter you hire. What matters is his track record of results for clients.

The reason track record is important is probably not what you think.

Yes, the placements this headhunter has made in the past demonstrate his competency.

More importantly, his placements have created a web of incred-ible relationships that he will network with to recruit the next star executive for your startup.

The bottom line is don't hire the nice, cool headhunter that feels like a warm bowl of chicken soup on a winter day. Hire the guy who is going to challenge you, make you think, and bring you the game-changer your startup needs now.

Reference Check the Recruiter

Don't work with a brilliant jerk. Verify that this recruiter is ethi-cal, honest, smart, listens, *and* brings results. Verify by asking the headhunter for his references.

Again, you don't need this recruiter to be Mr. Nice Guy who you plan to invite to your wedding. If you build that kind of relationship with him, wonderful! But what matters is you retain a headhunter who has great values.

The benefit is clear.

Good people hang out with good people. Star performers call back other star performers. So, when you find this exceptional recruiter, you can expect that the quality of candidates you meet will mirror his intellect, prowess, and fine reputation.

Negotiate Price

Most elite headhunters understand you are in startup mode and will empathize with your limited budget. Be prepared for them to say no to any type of "discounted fee" . . . but you should ask.

Here are five suggestions to take the sting out of the fee:

1. **Propose a flat fee.** This way you know exactly what your outlay of cash will be when you hire the star executive.

2. **Request a payment plan** that is paid ratably over twelve months rather than in 2–3 installments.

3. **Propose a performance plan** where most of the fee gets paid after the star executive has delivered on specific goals.

4. **Ask for a longer warranty period** on the placement.

5. **Ask for a discounted future search.** If you retain the headhunter again for a second or third search project, then you would request gentler fee terms.

All of these things should be asked for. Usually, the answer will be "no", but you may be surprised. Sometimes, you will get what you ask for, but it all starts with asking.

Make It Real

When you meet a star recruiter, invest in the relationship.

Make it real. It may be obvious, but let me explain why in a heartfelt way.

The best clients I have worked with made me feel recognized. They referred me to other founders. They said *thank you*. They invited me to their homes. I met their families.

They realized that cutting me a check felt good, but what was even better was making me feel that I delivered, did a good job, and that I belonged.

Yes, money is a strong motivator, but feeling that they matter is more important to elite headhunters. Kind of sappy, isn't it? Yet, top headhunters have exceptional emotional intelligence. They have depth and range to their feelings. They want to feel valued. We are human too.

Zooming out, it parallels how to recruit star executives:

Are you listening to them?

Are you showing genuine interest in *their story*? *Their lives*?

Do the same with an elite headhunter. Make him feel valued and listened to, then you win a friend for life.

You also gain access to their wisdom on all sorts of people issues—from their ability to help you background/reference check, to mirroring how they would have a delicate conversation with a co-founder who is not performing. The benefits are numerous.

To recap, you don't need to hire a headhunter if you master the techniques I've shared in this book. Of course, there may be times when a specialty niche–type hire is needed for your startup. In this case, a top headhunter can accelerate the search for this specific person. It will save you time, which is always more valuable than money.

Ironically, the secret to avoid paying fees for recruiting is to invest your time in copying what great headhunters do. Simple, isn't it?

That framework is now in your hands.

The rest is up to you.

CLOSING COMMENTS

Good work. You made it all the way to the end of this book. It is clear how much you care about building a remarkable company with incredible people.

It is my hope that I have provided you with the framework for elite recruiting.

Now the reps begin.

The muscle this book builds is not how to "out recruit" other founders. Instead, view it as a training manual for serving others. And the best way to serve others is to be present.

I know, I know. You are not reading this book for some repackaged self-help, New Age-y, spiritual reawakening pep talk.

You want to learn how to recruit at the highest level.

But the self-help gurus are right. They have built huge followings because they understand the basic human need for community, for belonging, for feeling that someone listens, and sincerely cares.

Not convinced? Let's go to Hollywood.

Ever meet an A-list celebrity? Can you imagine how hard it is for Brad Pitt and Taylor Swift to make a new friend?

It's the same challenge for a superstar CTO. Everyone wants to hire her, but who actually cares about *who* she is? My point here is that whether it is a Hollywood star or a star executive, we all want someone who listens to who we are, not just what we can do (for them).

Focusing on the "who" sitting before you in an interview is what separates founders who hire the best from founders who hire the rest (yes, it rhymes).

Interviewing is listening.

Listening takes presence. It takes energy. It takes heart.

When showing up as a focused listener who genuinely cares you become irresistible to the speaker.

Haven't we all met that person?

That is the person I want you to become. Do the reps.

Let me warn you with the obvious: star executives know they are important. They get paid well and are recognized constantly for their professional prowess. They achieved the best grades, 700+ GMAT scores, top MBAs, etc., but they are still like us, *human*.

They crave connection. We all do.

Once a star executive feels genuinely listened to, watch what happens next. Magic takes over, things get real, and the truth comes out.

Ironically, the truth they'll share may make it obvious they are not a fit for your startup. Be thankful either way.

Start with being present to recruit the best. It won't be easy. You will get distracted and stray from the path. You cannot be the best recruiter every day. But knowing this fosters inner patience and acceptance that "nothing memorable was built in a day."

However, by showing up and striving to be the best listener these game-changers have ever met, you seed a culture of elite recruiting and embody the mindset of a master builder. A builder of legendary teams.

Through your commitment to consistently follow the actions outlined in this book, you will hire, retain, promote, and build with the best. With such greatness by your side, imagine how good it will feel to not only fulfill your vision but do so with such incredible partners every step of the way.

Thank you for sharing your precious time with me. I cannot wait for you to thrive and teach others what you have learned here.

Here's to many more start dates with those remarkable executives who cannot wait to grow something special with the bold, beautiful, and generous person (and founder) you have always been.

My very best regards,
J. Patrick Gorman

Acknowledgments

What a pleasure to write this book. It was never in the plans to do such a thing, but then again neither did this Chicago guy dream he'd live in Silicon Valley, NYC, or Brazil. Certainly, never Brazil, but what a joy of an experience.

Many thanks to:

Joel Cummins, my best friend since we were twelve years old, who has been a constant inspiration. I thank you deeply for believing in me, encouraging me, and connecting me to the talented people who brought this book into reality.

Heather Prince, my talented and beloved sister, who has been a patient listener to my years of rambling. Your prowess in writing and poetry clearly brought this book to fruition.

J. Patrick Price, my editor, whose cool Chihuahua must be the inspiration for his literary gifts, keen eye, and outstanding work.

Jerome Letter, a dear friend, who continues to inspire me to think bigger and be better.

Clem Johnson, my mentor in recruiting, who taught me numerous lessons, including the most valuable one: trust yourself.

Christopher Kearney, my main boss at Arthur Andersen, who is masterful with people and inspired all of his teams by being genuine, real, and authentically himself.

Bob Fligel, Ed Fleischman, and Gary Grossman, as well as the talented team members at ExecuSearch in New York, who not only taught me the fundamentals of recruiting but also gave me invaluable life lessons I will always be grateful for.

My former business partner and our team at iFind Group, who taught me exceptional lessons in entrepreneurship, listening, teamwork, and humility.

Andrew Greier for your friendship, terrific attitude, deep listening, and thoughtfulness.

Fernando Andraus, Marcelo de Lucca, and the Michael Page team who hired me and taught me priceless lessons about the wonderful, magical country of Brazil.

Tadashi Shiraishi and Oscar Bosch whose excellence and commitment to their craft inspire me. But it's your kindness and generosity that continue to make me a better person (and friend).

R. Christopher Lund who defines wisdom, class, and leadership.

Gratitude to the various companies, authors, and speakers that inspired this book, including Carol Dweck, Dr. Robert Hogan, Corey Wayne, Adecco, Graham Duncan, Arthur Andersen, and countless others.

Finally, thanks to all the various founders who have endured collaborating with me over the last twenty years. I know it has not been easy, and I respect and cherish all the lessons you taught me on how to better serve you, as well as the next generation of founders. Future founders will unquestionably benefit from all the ups and downs we have experienced together. Know that I could not have helped others without your courage, patience, and generosity in working with me.

About the Author

J. Patrick Gorman was born and raised just outside the incredible city of Chicago where he quickly understood why Mike Ditka and the 1985 Chicago Bears were the greatest American football team in history. After graduating from the University of Notre Dame, he joined Arthur Andersen before moving to New York City where his work in executive recruiting began.

Starting in Manhattan and currently in São Paulo, Brazil, Patrick continues to support founders looking to hire the very best. He resides between Brazil and United States which really means he is waiting to be cast in the sequel to *Up in the Air* with George Clooney.

www.ingramcontent.com/pod-product-compliance
Lightning Source LLC
Chambersburg PA
CBHW070452090426
42735CB00012B/2520